TAROT MÉDIÉVAL

The Mysteries of the Initiate's Path

Translated and edited, with additional material by
CAITLÍN MATTHEWS

from the original text by
FRANCIS ROLT-WHEELER

With art recovered from the originals of Christian Loring by
WIL KINGHAN

REDFeather
MIND | BODY | SPIRIT

4880 Lower Valley Road, Atglen, PA 19310

Copyright © 2023 by Caitlín Matthews (text) and Wil Kinghan (illustrations)

Library of Congress Control Number: 2022944316

All rights reserved. No part of this work may be reproduced or used in any form or by any means—graphic, electronic, or mechanical, including photocopying or information storage and retrieval systems—without written permission from the publisher.

The scanning, uploading, and distribution of this book or any part thereof via the Internet or any other means without the permission of the publisher is illegal and punishable by law. Please purchase only authorized editions and do not participate in or encourage the electronic piracy of copyrighted materials.

"Red Feather Mind Body Spirit" logo is a trademark of Schiffer Publishing, Ltd.
"Red Feather Mind Body Spirit Feather" logo is a registered trademark of Schiffer Publishing, Ltd.

Designed by Brenda McCallum
Type set in Minion Pro/New Hero

ISBN: 978-0-7643-6620-8
Printed in China

Published by REDFeather Mind, Body, Spirit
An imprint of Schiffer Publishing, Ltd.
4880 Lower Valley Road, Atglen, PA 19310
Phone: (610) 593-1777; Fax: (610) 593-2002
Email: Info@redfeathermbs.com |
Web: www.redfeathermbs.com

To the memories of Francis Rolt-Wheeler
and Christian Loring

Out of heaven they shall cast not the day,
They shall cast not out song from the world.
By the song and the light they give
We know thy works that they live.

—Algernon Swinburne, *The Last Oracle*

ACKNOWLEDGMENTS

I am extremely grateful to Adam McLain for his kind help for getting us started. Thanks to Séverine Jeauneau for her support of this long-held dream project. A special thank you to Philip Graves of the Astrolearn Astrology Library for his help in providing copies of lost pages. I acknowledge the kind permission of Karen Mahony and Alex Ukolov to cite their article from http://magicbohemia.com. To Wil Kinghan for pouring himself into the challenging recovery of the artwork, great thanks for your skill and perseverance. Lastly, to John Matthews for his persistence in seeking out the *Tarot Médiéval* and helping to bring it to back to life. I know you wanted to work on this book, but commissions elsewhere prevented you. I hope you like it!

CONTENTS

INTRODUCTION: Reviving a Long-Lost Tarot	07
PART ONE The Original Text of *Tarot Médiéval* by Francis Rolt-Wheeler	13
CHAPTER 1. The Initiatory Path of the Major Arcana	18
CHAPTER 2. The Four Temples of the Minor Arcana	86
PART TWO Working with the *Tarot Médiéval* by Caitlín Matthews	145
CHAPTER 3. The Magical Background to *Tarot Médiéval*	146
CHAPTER 4. *Tarot Médiéval* in Action	180
Glossary	204
Notes	211
Bibliography	212

FIGURES

FIG. 1	An engraving made in 1608 of the Bembine Tablet, a first-century Roman depiction of Egyptian divinities	147
FIG. 2	The Otz Chaim or Tree of Life, here shown with the lightning flash	159
FIG. 3	A comparison of the ascription of Hebrew letters	162

FIG. 4	Major Arcana of Wirth-style Tarots on Tree of Life paths	163
FIG. 5	Major Arcana of Tarot Médiéval upon the paths	164
FIG. 6	The initiatory patterns of the Major Arcana	172
FIG. 7	The initiations of the Major Arcana	173
FIG. 8	The magical titles of the Major Arcana	175
FIG. 9	The sevenfold Ladder of Initiation in the Myth of Ishtar	177
FIG. 10	Hints for reading the pips from the Ten Sephiroth	183
FIG. 11	Keywords and qualities of the suits	184
FIG. 12	Roles and modalities of the court cards	185
FIG. 13	Example of a directional reading	188
FIG. 14	Directional reading with forward-facing cards	188
FIG. 15	Reading the story	191
FIG. 16	Example of reading the story	191
FIG. 17	The Judgement or French Cross spread	193
FIG. 18	An example of Judgement spread	194
FIG. 19	Weft of the Mysteries spread	196
FIG. 20	Example of the Weft of the Mysteries	198
FIG. 21	The Knights, Queens, and Kings reveal the date	201

INTRODUCTION

REVIVING A LONG-LOST TAROT

In 1940, the theater of the Second World War opened on yet another tragic act, as la Belle France—once the bastion of all things beautiful, elegant, and cultural—saw Paris finally fall to the invading Nazi forces. By June 22, the Vichy government of Marshall Pétain had come to terms with Germany, taking over from the Third Republic. The Nazi jackboot resounded through French streets as Hitler visited Paris just two days later—come to gloat over his victory and to ensure his iconic photographic opportunity in front of the Eiffel Tower. It was an image that spoke volumes to a defeated Europe. France the Fair had fallen, and with it vanished many beautiful things.

Tarot Médiéval by Francis Rolt-Wheeler and artist, Christian Loring was a Tarot published in the fateful year of 1939 in Nice, France. That printing seems to have not survived the fall of France in June 1940, and the very few copies that remain only exchange hands in auction houses, so rare is it now.

The British esotericist Francis Rolt-Wheeler (1876–1960) was an enterprising man. He ran away to sea at the age of twelve, embarking for the United States on a sailing ship. He worked as an editor for various US and Canadian newspapers and was later ordained as an Episcopalian priest. He lectured for the New York Board of Education, writing a series of boy's adventure books between 1916 and 1924, but from the late 1920s onward, his literary output concentrated upon esoteric studies. In 1923, he then traveled on to Tunisia, where he founded the Astrological Institute of Carthage. His long-running esoteric magazine L'Astrosophie was published from 1929 to 1958, with a wartime gap between June 1940 and September 1949. Rolt-Wheeler was a persevering presence among the European esoteric confraternity, disseminating esoteric ideas in his magazine.

Christian Loring's details have proved impossible to trace, and I have concluded it must be so because she kept a very low profile or, more likely, that this name was merely a pseudonym. Rolt-Wheeler writes of the artist as "a serious scholar and occultist," one learned in Kabbalah, and "a mistress of colour harmony," thus giving us the only clue to the artist's sex! Rolt-Wheeler collaborated again with Loring, who provided sensitive black and white illustrations for his book Mystic Gleams from the Holy Grail (1948). It was actually Christian Loring who put this Tarot in motion, for she had an exhibition of her Tarot images at the Autumn Salon in 1934. Her images at this annual art exhibition, held in the Champs-Élysées, clearly delighted Rolt-Wheeler, who wrote in the July 1935 issue of his magazine, L'Astrosophie (in which he started to serialize articles on the major arcana, accompanied by black and white renderings of Loring's cards):

"In a completely surprising and unexpected way, we were recently permitted to view a series of Tarot cards painted with great finesse and distinction by Christian Loring, exhibited at the Autumn Salon. The colours are beautiful and so subtle that it seems nearly impossible to render these Arcana into black and white. We have not lost hope that, one of these days, a lover of beauty and spiritual thought—perhaps one or more of our many readers—will reproduce this wonderful Tarot, leaving it as a legacy for future generations, or help us to do so, on a practical basis. This just the most beautiful set of Tarot cards in the world, for which it has been waiting this long time."

Clearly, Rolt-Wheeler somehow found the finances to publish the Tarot—possibly from his many subscribers to L'Astrosophie magazine—only to have it unfortunately swallowed up by the fortunes of war; it is possible that the whole edition and perhaps the original artwork also must have been destroyed at this time. While Rolt-Wheeler reprinted the articles and black and white images of the Tarot again in L'Astrosophie, he never again attempted to republish the Tarot Médiéval, whose rarity has now put it beyond the reach of all but the most exclusive Tarot collector.

We tend to think of the period between the publication of the Rider Waite Smith deck in 1909 and the Tarot explosion of the last fifty years as a kind of Tarot desert, but Tarot Médiéval helps to correct that assumption, showing that the period between the two world wars had its own vision. Tarot Médiéval stands between the era that saw the publication of the Rider Waite Smith deck in 1909, the Oswald Wirth Tarot des Imagiers of 1927, and Manley Hall's and J. Augustus Knapp's Knapp-Hall Tarot of 1929, and the era of commercial Tarot publication, which began in the 1970s.

Working from the printed text of Rolt-Wheeler's esoteric magazine, L'Astrosophie, and from other sources, I have translated Rolt-Wheeler's original text for each card from the French, while Loring's artwork has been recovered from photographs of the original card images by Wil Kinghan.

In translating Rolt-Wheeler's original, I have worked closely with the text, only removing any repetitive passages, and editing prolix expositions. Occasionally, I have also removed or edited passages where offense might be taken due to the outmoded views of men's and women's roles in society that occasionally appear in the text, and moved longer teaching paragraphs to part two, where the reader may have more leisure to study them.

The entries for each card explore their symbolic, initiatory, kabbalistic, numerological, astrological, and divinatory significances, with the stress being upon the spiritual life of the initiate. For the modern user, more accustomed to the divinatory meanings of each card being more prominent, I have included further divinatory suggestions: these are indicated by the use of "Also," showing that the following text is added. These amplifications come largely from the work of Etteilla, upon which the author drew. Rolt-Wheeler liked to be a completist, with his lists of magical and symbolic correspondences, sometimes equating disparate traditions in ways that now seem a little forced. This follows the fashion of the time, where traditional magical training was thin on the ground; the added assurance of being told "how to do it correctly" brought confidence to the avid student.

Please note that in his descriptions of each card, the author often mentions details that are not actually present in the image, or he describes them rather differently: I have retained these anomalies.

In part one, which includes the original text by Francis Rolt-Wheeler, any comments by myself are in a different font. In part two, I have provided a historical background so that readers may understand the lineage of this Tarot, as well as the magical and initiatory aspects of the Tarot that the author practiced. I have set aside my own Qabalistic ascriptions of cards to the Tree of Life in order to honor the Oswald Wirth school method that the author followed, giving a few methods of my own by which you might explore these connections a little deeper. A glossary of specialist exoteric terms and notes can be found on p. 202.

Rolt-Wheeler was deeply moved by the medieval vision, and by Christian Loring's images, which draw upon an idealized medieval world whose reminders can still be seen all over France. In the face of Europe's crisis, the author's medieval aesthetic and his spiritual devotion to the esoteric path sent its enchanting song into the heart of darkness, sounding as a clarion to return once again to the core values that uphold civilization.

Like the angel that blows its trumpet over the tombs in the Judgement card, this Tarot rises from the dead at a time when different challenges face us. May the vigor and courage with which Rolt-Wheeler maintained the initiate's path at a time when Europe was facing the challenges of war, enable us all to embody the high ideals of the Tarot Médiéval in our own times.

Caitlín Matthews
January–August 2021
Oxford

PART ONE

THE ORIGINAL TEXT OF *TAROT MÉDIÉVAL*

By Francis Rolt-Wheeler

Edited and translated by Caitlín Matthews

Every star has an individual name.
—Aryeh Kaplan, *Sepher Yetzirah*

INTRODUCTION TO THE TAROT MÉDIÉVAL

by Francis Rolt-Wheeler

The following foreword is taken from volume XIII, no 1 of L'Astrophie, dated July 1935, where Rolt-Wheeler introduces his readership to the Tarot cards painted by Christian Loring. At the time of writing this, he was unable to publish the Tarot, but had decided to issue each image with a commentary. Here, the author gives us his first impressions of Loring's work, as well as his own opinions about existent Tarots, and provides a hint to his own sources of research. CM

TO OUR READERS

The secrets of Tarot, the mysteries of the Rose Cross, the search for the Holy Grail, and the transmutation of the Philosopher's Stone are nothing but four different aspects of the same thing: the discovery and exploration of the sublime mysteries of the spiritual world. Of these four routes, the Tarot possesses the great advantage of being pictorial; but on the other hand, the pictorial and symbolic have been subjected to a terrible disadvantage, for their marvelous symbolism has been conveyed by drawings so grotesque, so badly made, and so unsubtle in their coloration that they are utterly unfitted to covey the Tarot's symbolic and spiritual teachings, almost making the student give up any such study, with cards that blunt any enthusiasm.

In a subtle and unforeseen way, I was recently given the opportunity to see a series of Tarot cards of great finesse and distinction painted by Christian Loring, who exhibited at the Autumn Salon. The coloration is splendid and so subtle that it seemed to us almost impossible to convey these cards in merely black and white. We maintain the hope that one of these days, a lover of beauty and spiritual thought—perhaps one of our many readers—will cause this marvelous Tarot to be left to the common heritage of future generations, or perhaps even give us the means to help us manufacture this Tarot. It is the only truly beautiful set of Tarot cards to exist in this world, one for which the world has been waiting for centuries. We are proud to be able to present for the first time this new artistic version of the Tarot. *Astrosophy* will reproduce the entire series of major and minor arcana as frontispieces in this magazine, month by month.

It is so rare to find in the same person an artist and painter endowed with such subtlety and charm, having a fine drawing style, and being the mistress of the harmonious nuances of color, while at the same time, a serious and learned esotericist. The readers of *Astrosophy* know well that we do not readily confer the title of "esotericist." Christian Loring is very advanced in her qabalistic studies, and I am certain that the great mysteries are not a closed book to her. We know that many of our readers will esteem her true artistic and occult value in the pictures that will appear here.

An interpretation of each arcana will be given in the last two pages of our magazine. It is perhaps permitted to say that these two monthly pages, when put together, will form an initiatory study on the Tarot, giving a large part of the teaching that has not been previously written down, having existed only as oral tradition. These interpretations will give a précis of the fuller lessons given in our extensive Qabala Course. We advise our readers to carefully keep these issues together until the end of the series.

It would not be just, on my part, to ignore the high worth of the work of other seekers along the same lines. Christian Loring has been inspired, while making many modifications, by the information given by the major arcana of Oswald Wirth in his book *Le Tarot des Imagiers du Moyen Age* or The Tarot of the Medieval Craftspeople, but, being a specialist in medieval art, she has liberated the Tarot from that somewhat rigid, gauche, and primitive style.

A complete modern Tarot with all the minor arcana in the form of pictures has been made by Miss (Pamela Coleman) Smith, under the direction of Mr. A. E. Waite in England, titled *A Pictorial Key to the Tarot*: its details are full of riches because Waite is the most eminent and learned, literary and eclectic of the nineteenth-century occultists; unhappily, the artist does not possess the sacred fire, and the cards fail to spiritually uplift. There also exists a German Tarot, made in the Egyptian manner, on very small cards that are useful for divination; but if the major arcana is not inspired, then one should not bother, and the minor arcana follow the tradition of figures and geometric symbols.[1] But for those who are seeking to deepen their knowledge along higher lines, the *Tarot Médiéval* will provide all the vibrancy that one seeks in divination.

The cards of the Tarot have been most fulsomely presented in detail, with all their magical, qabalistic, and zodiacal correspondences by "'Enel" in two books: *Trilogie de la Rota* (Trilogy of the Wheel) and *Manuel de Cabbale Practique* (Handbook of Practical Kabbalah), giving us the basis of a synthesis of both qabalistic and Egyptian systems; the study of these two books is virtually obligatory for those who would wish to deepen their knowledge of tarot.[2]

A recent work, *Le Tarot, les arcanes, la divination* by J. Maxwell, based upon the *Tarot de Marseille*, uses a great deal of numerology in its pages; this book has no images, but it presents a very good, concise study of the symbolism. A more precise study of the Tarot has been made by Jean Gaston Bourgeat (1864–1919) in his book *Le Tarot, aperçu historique* (Tarot, Glimpses from History), but the author is not a qabalist. Those who know how to extract the highest truths from the works of Eliphas Lévi will not overlook his book *Le Clef des Grands Mystères* (The Key to the Great Mysteries). Finally, not to leave out of our account our esteemed French popularizers, we will mention the two books of Papus (Dr. Encausse): *Le Tarot des Bohémiens* and *Le Tarot Divinatoire*; and *La Synthèse du Tarot* by George Muchery, the last of the independent cartomancers.

For those who read English, a really important book on this

topic was written by Dr Thierens: *A General Key to the Tarot*, where the treatment of astrology and theosophy is admirable; this book is distinguished by an independence of thought, associated with a profound knowledge of the topic. The greatest esotericist of our day, Dion Fortune (1890–1946), is at this moment preparing a work of great stature on the Mystical Tarot.[3]

This little bibliography shows all the books that are necessary for a study of Tarot, and it is astonishing to think that *Le Tarot Médiéval* by Christian Loring will become—for these systems—the most esoteric and artistic Tarot, because it is made by a soul who is immersed in the Mysteries. F.R.W

CHAPTER 1

THE INITIATORY PATH OF THE MAJOR ARCANA

The Shape of the Major Arcana in *TAROT MÉDIÉVAL*

Each card entry begins with the description of the card, and its initiatory and mythic significance on the path of the mysteries. This is followed by a series of symbolic correspondences, where the geometric solid or shape and the Hebrew letter are given with the numerological associations. Then the esoteric and exoteric astrology is given, as well as the requirements of working with the card in a magical ritual. The symbol upon the card is largely derived from *The Key to the Universe* and *The Key to Destiny* by Curtis.

The reader will notice that the order of the major arcana is the customary Milanese order to which we are now accustomed, with one notable exception: the positioning of the Fool, numbered XXI, now lies between XX Judgement and XXII The World. This has come about because Rolt-Wheeler was following the Oswald Wirth pattern, based upon the order of Éliphas Lévi, whose sequencing of the Hebrew letters the author follows here.

This is what Rolt-Wheeler says about the Fool:

"One of the great mysteries in the numeration and order of the major arcana is just what place the Fool takes within it: it is perhaps associated with zero, but also situated at XXI or again, with less justification, at XXII. In our interpretation of *Tarot Médiéval*, we are following the esoteric line, trying to maintain the meanings belonging to the true Kabbalah, which gives the letter Shin, the Messianic letter, the twenty-first place in the sacred alphabet, to this card. This determines the order of this card in the series. The use of the Fool in the position of zero is permitted, according to another tradition which is strictly exoteric."

To understand more about the background of *Tarot Médiéval,* see chapter 3. —CM

I MAGICIAN

I THE MAGICIAN
The Juggler

SYMBOL: a dot within a circle
HEBREW LETTER: א ALEPH

 We see a young man, indicating humanity "made in the mental image of God." He stands before a table on which lie three symbols, while the fourth is in his hand. These are the Scepter or Wand, corresponding to the element of air, also with Kether at the summit of the Tree of Life. The second is a double-edged sword, corresponding to fire and the solar sphere of Tiphareth. The third is a Chalice or Cup, corresponding to the water and the lunar sphere of Yesod. The fourth is a Shekel (pentacle or coin), corresponding to the Earth and the terrestrial sphere of Malkuth. These correspondences respectively establish the coordination of the Hermetic, Qabalistic, Alchemical, and Astrological arts. The left hand of the Magician is lifted, indicating that he receives his power from on high; he holds the magic wand in this hand. The right hand touches the Shekel, emblem of Earth, symbol of the spiritual force that exteriorizes in matter.

INITIATORY SIGNIFICANCE:

The Magician represents humanity, the microcosm which reflects the macrocosm, the creator-man, Adam Kadmon, the demiurge. The infinite possibilities of humanity are symbolized by the lemniscate (the horizontal 8) over the Magician's head; the lemniscate is the line between time and eternity. The four symbols of Scepter, Sword, Chalice, and Shekel indicate respectively, intuition (spiritual body), reason (mental body), emotions (astral body), and the physical body of the man. This card is rightly linked to Arcana XXI the Fool, as the beginning foresees the end.

SYMBOLIC CORRESPONDENCES:

The Magician corresponds to the first letter of the Hebrew alphabet, Aleph, one of the three mother letters. Its form reveals the Hermetic axiom "As above, so below," repeated in the Magician's gesture. In occult geometry, his symbol is a perpendicular line, the column, obelisk, and phallic objects, also as two oblique lines shown in an opposing way, but that never join up.

In numerology, its number is 1. We see one person, two ellipses, three symbols on the table, four elements, five sides on the base of the chalice, indicating the first magical succession of the five Tarot cards.

In magical operations, its name is "the Powerful Magician." The magical weapon is the wand. The color for rituals is yellow-orange. The perfume is white sandalwood. The precious stone is oriental topaz, the symbolic stone is agate. The creature which attends it is the eagle. The tree is the palm.

PRACTICAL DIVINATION:

Upright: The true significance of the magician is creation and will. Also, creative power, intelligence, activity, the good beginning of an affair.

Unfavorable or Reversed: Abuse of authority, scandal, sorcery, bad luck, and the bad beginning of an affair, also cheating, trickery.

II THE PRIESTESS
Papesse *or* The Female Pope

SYMBOL: a dot
HEBREW LETTER: ב BETH

 We see a Priestess seated on the tessellated pavement in the Temple of Solomon. She is crowned with a tiara with a crescent moon upon it. On her knees is a book on which are often inscribed the letters T. R. for "Torah," the secret doctrine of Israel; or Toth-Ra, the secret doctrine of Egypt; or Rota, the secret doctrine of Asia; and Tarot, the initiatory synthesis. The Priestess holds two keys, of iron and of gold, widely called the keys of hell and of heaven, but they are truly the keys of matter and of spirit. The two columns of Jachin and Boaz, indicating the principles of masculine and feminine, active and receptive, the two polarities without which no manifestation would be possible.

INITIATORY SIGNIFICANCE:

The Priestess indicates duality, in the same way in which Magician symbolizing unity. She is feminine because the Shekinah or the Glory of God is feminine. The first manifestation, the first Divine expression, cannot make anything except by the two polarities. The Catholic cult of the Virgin Mary shows that Christianity appeals to the feminine element of spiritual esotericism.

SYMBOLIC CORRESPONDENCES:

The Priestess corresponds to the second letter of the Hebrew alphabet, Beth, a double letter whose hieroglyphic meaning is "the mouth" or "the Word," for "in the beginning was the Word, and Word was with God, and the Word was God."

In occult geometry, the symbolism of the Priestess is represented by two parallel lines that never meet in the end, although they make the computation of infinity. The true union of masculine and feminine completes the spiritual plan. In numerology, the number is two, indicating the polarities, duality, vibration and life, because all life possesses a vibratory character.

In magical work, her title is "the Priestess of the Stars." The magical implement is the bow and arrow of Diana. The ritual color is luminous blue. The perfume is storax, the male fern, and the scent of forests at night. The precious stone is the opal, the stone where solar and lunar lights are combined; the symbolic stone is chalcedony. The beast is the sacred ibis. The symbolic tree is almond.

PRACTICAL DIVINATION:

Upright: Inspiration is the true meaning of the Priestess, wisdom, faithfulness, rest, mental and spiritual riches. Also, discretion, spiritual counsel, study.

Unfavorable or reversed: Passive resistance, unpaid work, superficial rationalisation, love of luxury. Also, secrecy, false revelation, spiritual credulity.

III THE EMPRESS
Isis-Urania *the* Cosmic Mother

SYMBOL a downward-pointing triangle
HEBREW LETTER ג GIMEL

 The Empress represents creative thought, the breath of life, the Spirit of the Trinity, and the spiritual mother of the cosmos. She is shown as a winged queen, seated in space. Twelve zodiacal stars form a halo over her head. Her feet are set upon a downward-pointing crescent moon. Oswald Wirth says: "This confirms her domination over the sublunary world, or all that is perpetually changing and ceaselessly transforming." Her blazon is the Falcon of Horus, while her scepter combines the symbol of two polarities. The lily is the symbol of the Virgin Mother, the falcon leads us to Isis, and the twelve stars to Urania.

INITIATORY SIGNIFICANCE:

The Empress signifies the realization of creative thought with the power of mental evocation; as Isis, she is the key to the mysteries of numbers, governing spiritual evolution; as Isis-Urania, she is the universe binding time and space together; as Cosmic Mother, she symbolizes the union of two polarities within her maternity, with the capacity of Nature to bear children, and a power of cosmo-biological evolution.

On a higher, initiatic plane, the Empress represents the balancing power acquired when the polarities are harmonized. As the Trinity of the Absolute, the Shekinah, and of Nature, she resonates with the male and the female aspirant, and the harmony of the great work. Spiritual development is able to create a man or a woman by polarity alone, but an initiatory working needs harmony, which is only possible when a third factor unites the two operators.

SYMBOLIC CORRESPONDENCES:

The Empress corresponds to the third letter of the Hebrew alphabet "Gimel," a double letter conveying the sense of action. This letter expresses the Holy Spirit in the sense of the Reviver of Nature, the Renewer of the Divine Breath, the Supreme Activity in every action.

In esoteric geometry, the Empress's symbol is an equilateral triangle, with its point above, signifying divine manifestation. The triangle is also the symbol of spiritual evolution, a form of the dynamic evolutionary spiral. In numerology, the number is three for the Trinity, the perfection of divine expression.

In magical operations, the title is "the Daughter of the Almighty." The magical implement is the belt. The color for rituals is emerald green, also black. The perfume is camphor. The precious stone is emerald; the symbolic stone is turquoise; the esoteric stone is star sapphire. The beast is the bird of heaven, the falcon. The symbolic tree is the hazel tree.

PRACTICAL DIVINATION:

Upright: The true meaning of the Empress is exteriorization or manifesting what is within. Power, health, achieving your wishes, solving difficulties. Also, harmony, nurture, and nature.

Unfavorable or reversed: Sterility, illness, clandestine actions, new annoyances, lack of harmony. Also, dependence and overprotectiveness.

IV THE EMPEROR
The King *of the* World • The Cubic Stone

SYMBOL: an upward-pointing triangle
with a cross under it

HEBREW LETTER: ד DALETH

 The Emperor or the King of the World, the Master of Materialization, is shown seated upon the Cubic Stone. He is the Greek Pluto and the Demiurge of the Platonists, resonant with Jehovah of the kabbalists, Lord of the seven lower sephiroth of Formation. The sign of Sulphur, which is the sign of a cross upon a triangle, is seen in the Emperor's posture, with his head and arms forming a triangle above, while his crossed legs make a cross below. In his left hand he holds a globe, divided by a hemisphere and two quarter- spheres; the globe is surmounted by a cross of six directions, symbolizing the unity of manifestation, the two polarities, the four elements, and the six directions of space. His scepter carries the crescent of illusion, terminating in a lozenge, the symbol of positive manifestation, with a cross, the symbol of sacrifice, and a fleur de lys, indicating the receptive polarity. The Cubic Stone, on which the Emperor is seated, stands for raw matter that has been sculpted by the conscious will. The black eagle on the stone contrasts to the white falcon on the Empress's shield. Stylized emblems of the Sun and the Moon on his chest indicate the work by day and by night.

INITIATORY SIGNIFICANCE:

This arcana indicates the transformation of the triad into a quarternity, or the passage of the Trinity into manifestation. The Emperor is the master of everything that is manifest, Lord of Matter; as King of the World, he receives the forces from the spiritual plans and transforms them for use on the earth. In the symbolism of the Cubic Stone, he indicates the Great Work, the Great Architect of the Universe, and the illuminated worker, dignified by his task. It is by the action of the spirit upon matter by which all matter becomes spirit again.

SYMBOLIC CORRESPONDENCES:

The Emperor corresponds to the fourth letter of the Hebrew alphabet: Daleth, a double letter, meaning a door, symbolising the double manifestation of form and principle by their mutual reactions upon the material and spiritual planes.

In esoteric geometry, the Emperor is indicated by the cross, or the spirit crucified upon matter; also by the lozenge of the involutionary and evolutionary triangles conjoined. In numerology, we see how matter finally returns to unity. The triad resounds within the quarternity, and there it stops. Adding up in this fashion: $1 + 2 + 3 + 4 = 10$ and also $1 = 0 = 1$, we touch upon the end of simple numbers and, finally, upon the Absolute.

In magical operations, the name is "the Chief of the Powerful." The magical implement is the burin (or sometimes the set square). The color for ritual is scarlet. The precious stone is the ruby. The animal is the ram.

PRACTICAL DIVINATION:

Upright: The true meaning of the Emperor is authority. Achievement, will, material success, physical power. Also, dynamism and stability.

Unfavorable or reversed: Tyranny, revenge. Also, inflexibility, authoritarianism.

V THE HIEROPHANT
The Initiator • The Pope

SYMBOL: a pentacle
HEBREW LETTER: ה HEH

 The Hierophant or Initiator is the guardian of the high secrets, while in medieval understanding, he is the pope, Patriarch of Rome—one of seven patriarchs of early Christianity who still survive. Today, we do not consider the pope as the sole initiator of Christianity: since the invention of printing, education does not rest exclusively in the hands of the Church, and the evolution of spirituality follows many different ways.

The Hierophant or pope is seated under an arch, symbol of the faith. The triple tiara upon his head indicates the three prerogatives of ecclesiastical work: 1. The church itself with its rites and ceremonies; 2. intellectual knowledge, with theology, mistress of the sciences, as its sovereign; 3. spiritual knowledge. His right hand is lifted in benediction. In his left hand he holds a cross with three bars, indicating his power in the words of Yetzirah, Briah, and Atziluth, while the sevenfold terminals of the cross indicate his temporal power, which is attuned to the seven sephiroth of creation, the seven planetary influences, the seven notes of the scale, etc. The two neophytes or postulants symbolize Faith and Reason.

INITIATORY SIGNIFICANCE:

This arcana indicates the quintessence of power, and the transmutation of the quarternary into the quinternary. This transmutation expresses itself so: Magician—a point in a circle without dimension; Priestess—a dimension, the truth; Empress—two dimensions, manifestation; Emperor—three dimensions, matter as a cube; Hierophant—four dimensions (three of space and one of time). This mystery is encoded in the sphinx where its wings signify spiritual learning, its bull-flanks the power to act, its human head for knowledge, its lion's paws the ability to seize spiritual opportunities, while its breasts represent service to humanity and spiritual will.

SYMBOLIC CORRESPONDENCES:

The Hierophant corresponds to the fifth letter of the Hebrew alphabet: Heh, a single letter, and the inspirational breath in the sacred name Yod-Heh-Vau-Heh, the breath of God upon the waters that forms the demiurgic creation and within Adam to convey the divine spark of life.

In numerology, the number five signifies magic, which is the power of spiritual processes upon matter, revealed by 1 + 4. An understanding of Nature can lead us to a perception of God, which is indicated by 4 +1. When the Trinity defeats duality, it is shown by 3 + 2, but when the polarities are necessary for the manifestation of the triad, we can demonstrate this by this mirroring sum of 2 + 3.

In magical operations, the name is the "Mage of Eternity." The magical implement is the horns. The color for rituals is bright orange. The precious stone is topaz. The animal is the winged bull.

PRACTICAL DIVINATION:

Upright: The true meaning of the Hierophant is acceptance. Inspiration, magic, protection, kindness, mystical alliance. Also, blessing and education.

Unfavorable or reversed: Receptive to bad influences, insincerity, the abuse of authority. Also, spiritual corruption or subversion.

VI THE LOVERS
The Two Paths

SYMBOL: Solomon's Seal
HEBREW LETTER: ו VAU

 The Lovers represents humanity at the crossroads of material and spiritual ways, or the Left and Right Hand Paths. We see a young man at a dividing path; to his right is a noble woman, a queen who offers to conduct him upon the royal road leading to her spiritual realm. To his left, we see a bold bacchante, who attempts to embrace the young man. Above them is the angel of retribution, ready to release his arrow if the man misuses his free will to follow the way of lust or negligence. In the Middle Ages, this arcana was often interpreted as a choice between conjugal love and dissolute relationships, but here we stress the choice of divine love and our soul's downfall.

INITIATORY SIGNIFICANCE:

The chief meaning is free will. Destiny gives us opportunities to exercise our own choice, whether it be the choice between married love or an affair, work or laziness, duty or negligence. The choice to accept or to refuse responsibility for our actions is ours. The dutiful queen contrasts here with the voluptuous woman to depict the choice of an honorable path of inspiration and altruism or a dishonorable path of frivolity and egotism. Esoteric teaching presents love as the incarnation of a soul in the birth of the desired child; in the magnetic polarity of the sexes, essential for human harmony, and a balanced life; in the purely spiritual connection between two people; as well as in the relationship with a guide upon the higher planes.

SYMBOLIC CORRESPONDENCES:

The Lovers corresponds to the sixth letter of the Hebrew alphabet: Vau, one of the letters of the Tetragrammaton. Vau is a profound mystery, being the bridge between being and non-being, between the principle of life and life itself, both connecting and dividing. Vau means "an eye," associated with the third eye or the pineal gland, and its interpretation is "choice."

In esoteric geometry this arcana is symbolized by a star with six points, composed of two interwoven equilateral triangles. The triangle with its apex above indicates the spiritual world; the triangle with its apex below indicates the material world. Without a point at the center, it represents choice and the difficulty of untangling material and spiritual principles.

In numerology, the number 6 shows itself as the choice between two trinities: $3 + 3 = 6$; as the polarity of the sexes blessed by the trinity: $3 \times 2 = 6$; and as the sexes on a purely material basis: $2 + 4 = 6$. Six is the number of the cube with six sides, but if these are extended, it forms the Cross of Sacrifice.

In magical applications, the name of his arcana is the "Oracle of Two Powerful Gods." The color is yellow. The precious stone is alexandrite. The bird is the magpie.

PRACTICAL DIVINATION:

Upright: The true meaning of the Lovers is choice, or free will. Discrimination, tests, love, devotion. Also, reciprocal love.

Unfavorable or reversed: Bad choices, infidelity, indecision, a moral decline. Also, vacillation, ambivalence.

VII THE CHARIOT
The Chariot *of* David

SYMBOL: cross of Lorraine
HEBREW LETTER: ז ZAYIN

 The Chariot indicates the victory of man over the material conditions of life, a choice that has been made, a battle won, serenity acquired. A young man crowned, dressed in a breastplate and carrying a scepter, stands upright in a triumphal chariot that is drawn by two spirited horses: one white, the other black. The chariot is cubic, indicating matter, but the canopy over it has a star, suggesting that the heavens help the one who acts by himself. On the front of the chariot is a winged globe over a spinning top, one of the symbols of polarity. We see that the black horse is stubborn and impetuous, indicating impatience, while the white horse is persevering in its duty.

INITIATORY SIGNIFICANCE

The Chariot shows the material victory to which the dutiful initiate is led by destiny; it is also the Chariot of David, a Hebrew name for the Great Bear, or the constellation of the seven stars that directs us toward the Pole star. This corresponds to the seven rishis of Hindu mythology, or the seven Elohim of Creation. The hero of the Chariot is neither an ascetic nor a saint, but a man who is the conqueror of the sphere where his daily duties are acted out.

SYMBOLIC CORRESPONDENCES

The Chariot corresponds to the seventh letter of the Hebrew alphabet Zayin, whose sign signifies the sword and the scepter. In kabbalistic tradition, seven is attuned to the Word, especially in the work of creation, creation being a spiritual action upon proto-matter.

In esoteric geometry, the most important symbol is the triangle upon a square, or a pyramid upon a cube, an indication that for those who live on earth, manifestation is a means by which we understand divine truths.

In numerology, seven is the perfect and indivisible number, material perfection, the permanent connection established between the supreme power and its manifestation. In seven, the divine 3 leads us to the material 4, and the material 4 leads us to the divine 3. The is no equality between them, which would lead us into dualism.

In magical operations, the name of this arcana is "the Lord of Triumph and Light." In a spiritual sense, the stone that accompanies it is emerald, and in a material sense, it is amber. The color for ritual is amber, or less often green. The magical implement is the furnace or fire. The creature is the tortoise.

PRACTICAL DIVINATION:

Upright: The true meaning of the Chariot is victory, or more exactly, victory over oneself. Also, triumph, success, honors, the accomplishment of wishes.

Unfavorable or reversed: Remorse, an unremitting struggle, loss of legal case, shame, and a slave to bad habits. Also, lack of control and overconfidence.

VIII JUSTICE
The Sword *and* Balances • Themis

SYMBOL: Seal of Solomon: two intertwined triangles.
HEBREW LETTER: ח CHETH

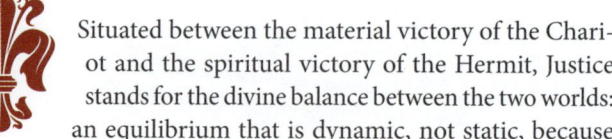 Situated between the material victory of the Chariot and the spiritual victory of the Hermit, Justice stands for the divine balance between the two worlds: an equilibrium that is dynamic, not static, because all life is in oscillation. The balances symbolize impartiality, and the sword both severity and protection. We see a woman of beautiful presence seated upon a throne. A crown of iron is on her head, having eight fleurs de lys, the emblem of justice. She holds the balances in her left hand, with the two pans standing equal. In her right hand she holds a great sword, with point lifted, ready to strike any who seek spiritual advancement at the expense of another. The sword of Justice is raised to protection the innocent, held by the arm of charity.

INITIATORY SIGNIFICANCE:

The initiatory teaching is based upon authority and order, against the chaos of anarchy and disorder. The duty of Justice is to strike anarchy upon earth and to punish impiety or antagonism to spiritual forces; also, to weigh in the balance not only the personality or exterior character of a human being, but also the individuality of the inner character. We each have to overcome the Guardian on the Thresholds before Justice permits the candidate to pass toward the ninth arcana.

SYMBOLIC CORRESPONDENCES:

Justice corresponds to the eighth letter of the Hebrew alphabet, Cheth, whose hieroglyphic meaning is a fence, or signifying the field of wheat. These two meanings demonstrate that whoever does not work cannot expect to harvest. Kabbalism teaches that the first commandment of God to humanity is the order to work;

laziness is blasphemy, and lying is both a personal and social shame.

In esoteric geometry we find two forms: the octagon and the two squares. The octagon means harmony, which is the chief end of Justice; two squares of the same size, superimposed gives us a star of eight points, indicating solar authority; a square placed diagonally in another square indicates the two worlds: the square is the material and the lozenge is the spiritual world, guarded by the four Regents of the four cardinal points, symbolized by four right-handed triangles.

In numerology, 8 is the cube of 2: 2 x 2 x 2, or the polarities expressed in the sense of divine justice. The Gnostics gave this number to the Pleroma or the fullness of heaven.

In magical operations, the name of this arcana is the "Daughter of the Lords of Truth." The color is a greenish yellow. The magical object is the ritual ordeal. The symbolic creatures are the sphinx and the tortoise.

PRACTICAL DIVINATION:

Upright: The true meaning of Justice is judgement or more exactly, the discrimination of balance. Also, recompense, truth, a new opportunity, satisfaction, harmony, restoration.

Unfavorable or reversed: Losses, scandals, disharmony, disillusion. Also, unfairness, prejudice, persecution.

IX HERMIT

IX THE HERMIT
The Veiled Lamp • The Wise Man

SYMBOL: an equal-armed cross.
HEBREW LETTER: ט TETH

 This is the card of spiritual victory and initiation. It is not the man of the world who carries the light here, but the solitary sage. We see an old man who walks with a stick, but with vigor and dignity. Dressed in the philosopher's cloak, both ample and sober in color, he holds aloft in his right hand a hexagonal lamp, which is divided horizontally by four bars, forming thirty light squares of light which, with the hexagons above and below, signify the thirty-two paths of Wisdom. With this lamp, he illuminates his own path, shining it equally upon the road of those who are on his left, but a fold of his cloak veils the lamp from those who are not ready to receive it, or who do not follow the way. He holds a stick with seven knots, making nine with the handle and the tip, symbolizing spiritual perfection.

INITIATORY SIGNIFICANCE:

The principal meaning of this card is initiation. An initiate requires three things: a theoretical knowledge of spiritual evolution; of the role humanity plays in this evolution; a working knowledge of esoteric principles with an ability to travel on the spiritual planes. This is the work of an initiate, whose true role is that of instructor, just as the role of a true priest is that of mediator.

SYMBOLIC CORRESPONDENCES:

The Hermit is in harmony with the ninth letter of the Hebrew alphabet, Teth, meaning "a roof." This number corresponds to the central power of the seven chakras of the east.

In esoteric geometry, we note that this ninth figure does not belong to matter. No substance crystallizes into a solid with nine facets, so there is no symmetrical form within geometry with nine faces. We have to take three triangles 3 x 3, where the form of an equilateral triangle with a point at its center and its lines that joins the center to form a W.

In numerology, 9 requires a study all of its own. In arithmetic, it is the controlling figure, divisible by nine. It ends the series of figures because a new cycle begins with ten. In symbolism it is the square of three, and the highest teaching.

In esoteric astrology, this arcana is associated with the sign of the Lion and the Sun. In esotericism, the Sun is the distributer of the life spiritual, which is exactly the role of the Initiate.

In magical operations, the name of this arcana is "the Prophet of Eternity"; and also "the Magician of the Word of Power." The color for rituals is a clear yellowish green. The magical object is the lamp. The animal is the antelope.

PRACTICAL DIVINATION:

Upright: The true significance is initiation, acceptance, spiritual victory. A critical success, material losses, ostracism, solitude.

Unfavorable or reversed: Weakness, a fall from grace, condemnation, a monastic life. Also, depression, asceticism, obstacles, and delay.

X THE WHEEL of FORTUNE
The Wheel *of* Life • The Sphinx

SYMBOL: a round dot
HEBREW LETTER: ׳ YOD

 This arcana shows a wheel with two rims, representing the hurly-burly of life. The eight spokes of the wheel form a material cross of equal arms, and a spiritual cross in the form of a St. Andrew's Cross. These two forces, totalling 8, come into balance in arcana VIII. Two figures hang onto the rim of the wheel; on the ascending side we see Hermanubis, representing birth and rebirth, experience, tests; he carries the caduceus of wisdom and healing; cast down on the descending side, we see Typhon or Set, representing death, destruction, collapse, winter. Above we see the Sphinx, motionless, sword in hand, characterising Destiny. The Wheel is forever turning, indicating free will, because humans seek to mount with Hermanubis or descend with Typhon. The wheel floats on the Ocean of Chaos, supported by a double lunar crescent, symbol of Cancer.

INITIATORY SIGNIFICANCE:

This arcana begins a new series of numbers with a new order of idea. The first nine arcana touch upon the interior life of the neophyte; the nine following arcana reveal the active life of the Initiate. (see p. 172) Once initiation has been received, the law is inviolable: "whoever gives nothing receives nothing more."

SYMBOLIC CORRESPONDENCES:

The deepest teaching of this arcana is associated with the ten sephiroth or divine emanations that direct the continual creation of the worlds, a study requiring many years of study to understand and use in an esoteric way. The Wheel of Fortune corresponds to Yod, the tenth letter of the Hebrew alphabet, symbol of the germ of life. This letter is the architectural basis for all the letters of the sacred alphabet, and the first manifestation of the Word.

In esoteric geometry, the symbol is that of Yin-Yang, or the circle divided into two parts, one white, one black, by a spiral line, with a dot of the opposing color in the opposite sides. This double curve is conveyed by 5 x 2, because the curved spiral = 5. The Yin-Yang symbolism is a living polarity, and it is used as a symbol of reincarnation. In esoteric numerology 10 is the beginning of a cycle, as well as the return to unity or $1 + 0 = 1$.

In exoteric astrology, this arcana corresponds to Capricorn, ruled by Saturn, Set, or winter; and in esoteric astrology, it is Virgo, the Rose of Sharon, "the daughter all beautiful within," and in a Messianic sense, the Shekinah. In magical operations, the name of this arcana is "the Lord of the Powers of Life." The color for rituals is violet. The magical object is the scepter or wand. The incense is saffron. The animals attributed to this card is the winged sphinx.

PRACTICAL DIVINATION:

Upright: The true meaning of this arcana is responsibility, karma, destiny, fortune, luck, change, activity, the need to act decisively.

Unfavorable or reversed: Collapse, fall, bad luck, mischance, shaken by circumstances

XI STRENGTH
The Tamed Lion • The Muzzled Lion

SYMBOL: a Seal of Solomon
HEBREW LETTER: כ KAPH

 This arcana is the first of a series about the Initiate's actions toward others, showing clearly that the most powerful force that acts upon others is that of moral influence.

The symbolism of this arcana shows a crowned queen, with the lemniscate of spiritual power over her head, holds apart the jaws of a ferocious lion. The gesture is made without any apparent force, with a moral power that is without ceremony.

INITIATORY SIGNIFICANCE:

According to esoteric teaching, moral force operates within society to which each person bears their own responsibility. An initiate's life is lived with a more concentrated morality, having obligations toward the invisible fraternity of which he or she is a part. By linking your own development with your progress within the order and discipline of the invisible fraternity, with your progress under the inspiration of beings of a higher plane, you become part of a golden chain linking your soul to the Divine Soul, which is made up of a succession of initiatory colleagues in esoteric orders and hierarchies, even to the celestial spheres. All members of that chain must uphold morality lest the whole group would go into a decline.

SYMBOLIC CORRESPONDENCES:

Strength corresponds to Kaph, the eleventh letter of the Hebrew alphabet, whose hieroglyphic meanings is a hand taking another hand. This symbol, "the Hand which holds the Hand of God," is a common symbol in esoteric orders. In esoteric geometry, the symbol is that of a star with five points found in the central hexagon formed by a star of six points, or the Seal of Solomon.

The meeting of these two stars is actually the symbol of the magical power of an initiatory order and is not to be used by a single initiate. It also represents the intercalary days, or the eleven days that distinguish a lunar year of 354 days from a solar year of 365 days.

In esoteric numerology, XI signifies the curve of a spiral, the new beginning of unities in the divine plan. This number shows an initiatic character especially in its multiples; 22 are the major arcana of the Tarot; 33, the highest degree in Freemasonry; 44. the mystical Gnostic number; 77, "the perfection of perfections"; 99, the names of Allah.

In exoteric astrology, the eleventh arcana corresponds to Aquarius, ruled by Uranus, the octave of the Sun, the planet that rules occult orders. In esoteric astrology, Strength corresponds to the planet Mars in his feminine aspect, and with the Queen of Swords.

In magical operations, the name of this arcana is "the Daughter of the Lords of Truth," because nothing is stronger that truth. The color for rituals is emerald green. The magical object is the equal armed cross. The incense is galbanum with cloves. The animal is the elephant.

PRACTICAL DIVINATION:

Upright: The true meaning of this arcana is moral force, or simply strength. Also, courage, calmness, authority, self-control.

Unfavorable or reversed: Disloyalty, boastfulness, cruelty, abuse of power. Also, weakness, self-sabotage, and manipulation.

XII THE HANGED MAN
Sacrifice • Redemption

SYMBOL: a downward equilateral triangle surmounted by a cross.

HEBREW LETTER: ל LAMED.

 We see a beam, balanced between two tree trunks, each with six knots, creating a gallows on which a young man hangs by his left foot. He is in pain, but he is also accepting. Under each arm is a money bag from which coins fall continuously. His right leg is crossed under the other, and with his two elbows thrust out, giving him the shape of the Seal of Solomon, with its two interlaced triangles. The drawing also contains the symbol of the Achievement of the Great Work: an equilateral triangle with its point below, surmounted by a small cross.

INITIATORY SIGNIFICANCE:

As in the myth of Oedipus or of Christ, the initiate must sacrifice him or herself, not only in earthly matters giving up our accumulated treasures, but also the gold of wisdom and the silver of good deeds that are poured upon others; even if our body is immobilized, our spirit is still free. In the story of Hercules, twelve labors are accomplished, but he becomes a prisoner at the end of them; like Prometheus, he takes fire from heaven for the use of humanity, only to be chained to a rock and tormented. We see the transformation of evil into good in this arcana.

SYMBOLIC CORRESPONDENCES:

The Hanged Man corresponds to the twelfth letter of the Hebrew alphabet, Lamed, a single letter meaning "an arm," or an ox-goad, demonstrating the action of prayer.

In esoteric geometry, we have a zodiacal circle, with its four triplicities superimposed upon it: with earth, water, fire, and air creating a double Seal of Solomon. As a geometric solid, it is a dodecahedron, a fundamental form in the process of crystallization.

In numerology, this arcana shows us one form, two money bags, the triangle of power, four colors, five pieces of money, six points of the Seal of Solomon, seven points on the triangle and cross, for the achieving of the Great Work, eight tresses of hair, nine representing the initiation of 6 + 3, ten coins of gold and silver, and twelve knots on the trees signifying the zodiacal signs.

In esoteric astrology, arcana XII is associated with Pisces, the mystic sign of sacrifice. In exoteric astrology, the attribution is to Libra, the point of balance between reason and faith.

In magical operations, the name of this arcana is "the Spirit of the Powers of Water" or "the One Who Hangs Between Heaven and Earth." The color for ritual is a dark blue. The magical implement is the Chalice of Pain. The incense is myrrh. The beasts attributed to this card are usually found together: the eagle and the serpent, while the plant is the lotus.

PRACTICAL DIVINATION:

Upright: The main meaning of this card is sacrifice. Also, reflection, the will, devotion, charity, prophecy, prayer.

Unfavorable or reversed: Useless sacrifice, unrequited love, disgrace, remorse, and exile.

XIII DEATH
The Skeleton *with the* Scythe

SYMBOL: Saturn
HEBREW LETTER: מ MEM.

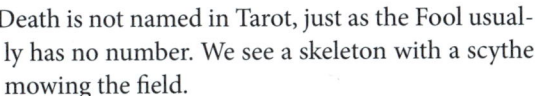
Death is not named in Tarot, just as the Fool usually has no number. We see a skeleton with a scythe mowing the field.

Among the fallen grain lie human heads, one of which is crowned, for neither riches nor rank count under the scythe of Grim Reaper. Behind the skeleton, we see hands and feet scattered on the earth. Each hand makes a gesture of friendship or blessing, except one downward grasping hand. Where Death has already passed, he gives life to hands ready to serve and bless, and to feet ready to run and help.

INITIATORY SIGNIFICANCE:

Survival after death has always been a doctrine among initiates. The idea of this mortal life being the end of everything is found only among the atheistic Greek Sophists and the rationalist "men of science." Life after death is not necessarily a return to this earth. The life of humanity upon earth is but a stage in a long series of lives through which the Divine Spark passes during the involutionary cycle to spiritualize again the material body. Each of its cycles are but a stage in the spiritual evolution of the cosmos.

SYMBOLIC CORRESPONDENCES:

Death is nothing but a door to the Afterlife, or a door to rebirth. The thirteenth arcana is associated with the Hebrew letter, Mem, which means "the mother" or "birth," and also "the sea." Mem is one of three mother letters.

In esoteric geometry, thirteen is the circle of the zodiac, with the earth at its center, the earth being known by the title "the Sorrowful Planet" because its trials of work and sacrifice are hardest.

In numerology, the "appeal of Black Magic" is symbolized in the shaping of 4 +5 + 4 =13, which is not to be used unwisely, or evil will befall. We also note the thirteen lunar months in a year of twelve solar months, and the third hierarchies of the Qlippoth or dark forces that mirror the Tree of Life.

In exoteric astrology, Death is associated with the planet Saturn or Cronos, who is always represented with a scythe. Saturn is the judge of the living and the dead; he is also "the Bridge which crosses the Abyss of Shadows." In esoteric astrology, this arcana is attuned with the watery triad, the subconscious plane of the Personality is ruled by Cancer and the Moon.

In magical operations, the name of this card is "the Lord of the Gate of Death," and also "the Child of the Great Transformers." The color for rituals is a greenish metallic blue, symbolizing corruption. The magical object is the lancet, and a flail that has points of flame. The incense is opoponax with a few grains of sulphur. The creatures attributed to this card are the beetle, the scorpion, and the crayfish; the plant is the cactus.

PRACTICAL DIVINATION:

Upright: The meaning of this arcana is death or end of something, transmutation, disillusion, discovering, the end, separation, agony.

Unfavorable or reversed: Actual death, disaster, a necromancer. Also, stagnation, resistance to endings or completions.

XIV TEMPERANCE
The Two Jars

SYMBOL: Aquarius—two rows of waves
HEBREW LETTER: נ NUN

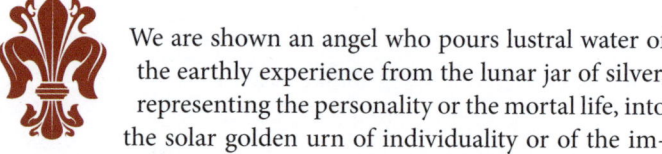 We are shown an angel who pours lustral water of the earthly experience from the lunar jar of silver, representing the personality or the mortal life, into the solar golden urn of individuality or of the immortal soul. In Hermetic symbolism, this represents the cycle of the universal energy. It is also the symbol of healing in spiritual therapy.

INITIATORY SIGNIFICANCE:

This card shows the transference of the mortal life of individuality, that part of us that links us to our chain of lives. The consecrated wine of the sacrament, the living divine water, and the forgetful draught of the river Lethe are all found in this symbol. While this card always means temperance or moderation, it has nothing to do with asceticism. Temperance means a true balance between spiritual and material things. We could wax fanatical about questions of diet, drink, sexuality, religion, or politics, but one is not better than the other. Balance requires us to be self-controlled, to have the self-governance to do the right thing.

SYMBOLIC CORRESPONDENCES:

This card is associated with the fourteenth letter of the Hebrew alphabet, Nun, whose meaning is "the Great Fish," also associated with Leviathan, a symbol of sexuality. Kabbalists have always insisted on a normal married life, as a celibate person is regarded as an offence to the Almighty. In esoteric geometry, this symbol is shown by each jar representing seven. Another geometric form is the Seal of Solomon, with the point at the center that marks the equality between the interlocking triangles.

In numerology, fourteen is called "the Key of the Circle,"

creating a connection between the diameter and the circumference of the circle, where Pi = 3.1415, whose numbers add up to 14. All the multiples of the number seven possess important means: This is also a lunar symbol, with fourteen days of the waxing moon, and waning moon. In kabbalistic practice, the first and third lunar weeks are spent in acts of charity, while the second and fourth weeks were given over to acts of justice.

In exoteric astrology, this card is associated with the planet Mercury, in his aspect of Hermes. Hermes is the key "to the seventh gate of the second world."

In esoteric astrology, this card is associated with the sign of Scorpio, which governs the sex of human beings and the secrets of nature.

In magical operations, the name of this arcana is "the Daughter of Reconciliation" and sometimes "the Light of the Door of Life." The color for rituals is light blue. The magical object is the bow and arrow. The incense is the resin made with the dried leaves of the water lily. The animal is the centaur and the hippogriff and, according to certain authors, the dog. The plant is the bullrush.

PRACTICAL DIVINATION:

Upright: The meaning of this card is temperance or moderation, and action, effort, balance, good health. Also, self-restraint, reconciliation, and conscience.

Unfavorable or reversed: Loss of opportunity, coldness, sexual perversion, illness. Also, excess, addition, and hedonism.

XV THE DEVIL
Typhon • Baphomet

SYMBOL: a downward-pointing pentacle
HEBREW LETTER: ס SAMECH

 This card shows a billy goat or devil crouched upon an altar. It has batwings symbolizing the darkness of night and hidden things; its cloven hooves represent bestiality. The generative organs are represented here as by a caduceus. In his left hand, Typhon holds a sexual symbol of the lingam and yoni; in the right hand is a downward-pointing torch of hate and destruction. Two human forms, male and female with horns, symbolizing the misuse of their natural powers and health, are chained to the altar or to each other.

INITIATORY SIGNIFICANCE:

The temptations attributed to Typhon concern normal sensuality that has been exaggerated by reading pornography or by aphrodisiacs. Baphomet's temptations touch upon a depraved sexuality, upon unnatural practices in the pursuit of a false occult power. The Devil's temptations replace creativity with scepticism, materialism, the negation of the existence of evil, as well as in envy and hate.

SYMBOLIC CORRESPONDENCES:

The fifteenth arcana is in rapport with the fifteenth letter of the Hebrew Alphabet, Samech, symbolising the snake and the fiery serpent. The devil's magical and harmful force moves by the power of degraded sexuality.

In occult geometry, Arcana 15 is the black point, depicted by a small black circle from which 15 curved hyperbolic lines ray out.

In numerology, the number is composed of 10, the number of the Wheel of Life, and 5, the number of magic itself. Apollonius of Tyana called it "the whirlpool of fear." The magic square of Saturn is based upon number 15; at the sorcerer's sabbat, the participants are not complete without the arrival of the "devil's representative." We find it also in the equation 5 x 3 by which human magic seeks to insult the trinity, whereas in 3 x 5 the divine force is able to elevate the human power.

In exoteric astrology, this arcana is associated with the planet Mars, planet of passion and desires; but Mars is the cosmic generator as much as humans. In esoteric astrology, this arcana is associated with Sagittarius and the centaur Chiron, half beast, half man, the great initiator, but belonging to the coarse and often bestial race of centaurs, if we recall the battle of the centaurs with Hercules. He teaches immortality, but he is not immortal himself.

In magical applications, the name of this arcana is "the Lord of the Gates of Matter" and "the Son of the Forces of Time." The color for these rites is black. The tool or magical symbol is the lingam and yoni. The incense or perfume is musk and Civet, with orchis root. The animal is the billy goat; the plants are thistle and hemp.

PRACTICAL DIVINATION:

Upright: The meaning of this arcana is temptation and evil or sensuality. It is enchantment, magic, passion, fascination, perversion, rebellion, hysteria, and abuse of power.

Unfavorable or reversed: Succumbing to evil suggestions, trapped in a web of coercion. Also, force majeure, bondage, and entanglement.

XVI THE LIGHTNING-STRUCK TOWER
The God-House • Fire *from* Heaven

SYMBOL: Mars
HEBREW LETTER: ע AYIN

 The ancient title of this arcana, "la Maison-Dieu" or the God-House, refers to the medieval Church whose ecclesiastical influence prevented any liberalism but whose organisation was exactly required for the era until the Renaissance. We see a tower of bricks or cut stones standing alone in the middle of a vast deserted plane. A streak of lightning symbolizing Divine Truth strikes the tower, demolishing it; two people are thrown from the balcony of the tower onto the ground below.

INITIATORY SIGNIFICANCE:

Three different forms of spiritual pride can be discerned within this arcana: those who try to turn the world to their own making: reformers, fanatics, vain healers, rigorous ascetics, deranged yogis, mediums with a pretended divine mission. Then those who desire to abolish the entire system, to put both general and soldier, boss and employee on the same level—leading to a world of social compromise. And those who wish to eliminate God in order to accentuate human values, where the poor victims of this "liberation" believe themselves to be little gods themselves. Pride enables them all to climb their tower, but Divine Truth ensures that their tower will be struck down by lightning.

SYMBOLIC CORRESPONDENCES:

This arcana is attuned to the sixteenth letter of the Hebrew alphabet, Ayin, which is interpreted as "the lunar powers," an ancient term that refers to when spiritual gifts are used by rational egoists.

In esoteric geometry, the symbol is that of the black magic square, or sixteen small black squares arranged in the form of a square.

In numerology, the figure 16 is a square of 4, the number of matter. At King Belshazzar's feast there were 16 noblemen, while the king had 16 golden balls upon his crown.[4] The equation of this arcana 2 x 8 gives us injustice or unbalanced justice, or divine wrath.

In exoteric astrology, this card is associated with the Moon, but since the eighteenth-century discovery of the planet Uranus, the Tower is now associated with it. This planet governs new, often bizarre, ideas, and is associated with a proud disdain for traditions. In esoteric astrology, this card is attuned with Capricorn, the characteristic sign of secret ambition, self-importance, and cold pride.

In magical operations, the magic name of this arcana is "the Lord of Proud Armies." The color for rituals is scarlet. The incense is dragon's blood with dried grains of pepper. The magical instrument is the sword. The animal associated with this card is the zebra and the wolf; the plants are absinthe and rue.

PRACTICAL DIVINATION:

Upright: The chief meaning is pride. Also, presumption, ambition, an insatiable appetite, brutality, grandstanding, and lack of balance.

Unfavorable or reversed: Timidity, failure to risk or dare, heaviness of spirit, maintaining a humble position despite the collapse of others around you.

XVII THE STAR of THE MAGI
The Stars • Optimism

SYMBOL: 8-pointed star
HEBREW LETTER: פ PEH

 We see a beautiful woman, kneeling by the banks of a river, with a vase in each hand, from which she pours out the contents. She represents virginity and maternity at the same time, being both Madonna and Vestal. The vases symbolize the two polarities: on the earth she pours the principle of masculine powers; into the water, the principle of the feminine powers. A great star, surrounded by seven small stars, shines over the woman's head. On one side is a bush of acacia, on the other the rose of sacrifice.

INITIATORY SIGNIFICANCE:

Initiation demands the exercise of the two polarities: the masculine polarity that manifests the divine power, exteriorizing itself as spirit and intelligence; the feminine polarity that exteriorizes and manifests in the soul and in beauty. The great star signifies the Pole Star, "the Sun of the Suns," with the Seven Rishis of the Great Bear around it. It is in rapport with Hope, and the Shekinah, the feminine glory of the Divine. Hope leads us to a healthy and beautiful life, lifting us from the material to the spiritual world, where supreme beauty is found. Sarcasm, cynicism, irony, critical malice, even the petty-minded materialism of small minds, severs all access to the Star of the Magi.

SYMBOLIC CORRESPONDENCES:

The seventeenth arcana corresponds to the Hebrew letter Peh, whose shape is a mouth with a tongue. It resonates with Hermes and with the two polarities of masculine thought and feminine word.

In occult geometry, the symbol is the isosceles triangle superimposed upon the equilateral triangle, the two triangles having the same base. The isosceles triangle signifies the two polarities, which are not able to act unless they are superimposed upon the equilateral triangle, the divine triangle.

In numerology, the sum of the ten sephiroth, acting with the four worlds of Atzilith, Briah, Yetzirah, and Assiah, and the three primordial emanations of Ain, Ain-Soph, and Ain Soph Aur make 17. Seventeen has 7 = material perfection and 10 = the beginning of the work for others on the Wheel of Life.

In exoteric astrology, this arcana is attuned to the planet Venus. In esoteric astrology, this arcana is governed by Mercury in his aspect of Hermes, the winged messenger of the goes, one of the leaders of the Army of the Voice, and a Prince of one of the Celestial Hierarchies.

In magical applications, the magical name of this arcana is "the Daughter of the Firmament" and sometimes, "that which lives between the Waters." The color for rituals is violet. The incense is galbanum, with laurel leaves. The magical tool is the censer. The animal attributed to this card is the eagle and the man, while the tree is the olive tree.

PRACTICAL DIVINATION:

Upright: The chief meaning of this arcana is hope, also, spiritual gain, the soul in peace, birth, optimism, worthy work, little material gain.

Unfavorable or reversed: Being misunderstood, impatience, despair, pessimism. Also, lack of faith, neglect of the soul.

XVIII THE MOON
Twilight • The Ordeals *of* the Moon

SYMBOL: a small circle over a
downward-pointing triangle

HEBREW LETTER: צ TZADDI

 This card shows us a dry, deserted landscape; it is the end of twilight, the light of the crescent moon is already stronger than that of the day. A path winds through this deserted place; it passes between two towers representing the guardians of the unknown; the path is lost in the distance. The Moon, which illumines the path, lets falls 32 drops, which indicate the dangers upon the 32 paths of wisdom. To the left of the road is a dog, emblem of flattery; to the right is a wolf, emblem of enmity, which howls at the moon. In the foreground is a dark pool, from which arises a crayfish, emblem of the basal instincts of humanity.

INITIATORY SIGNIFICANCE:

This is the last of the great ordeals that precede the second initiation. The neophyte needs to cross this vast desert, despite the pillars of excessive ambition and of discouragement that threaten from every side. The neophyte has to conquer the three flatteries of the dog: the false friends with hidden motives, one's own sense of self-satisfaction, and the temptations that seek to ground one. Then the neophyte must conquer the three hostilities of the wolf: the false-faced enemy, the cruelty within oneself, the intimidations of evil. Last, the neophyte must overcome the three temptations of the crayfish: the values of family, class, or race; the iron manacles of life's habits; the creeping sensuality that lurks near the surface.

SYMBOLIC CORRESPONDENCES:

This card is attuned with the eighteenth letter of the Hebrew alphabet, Tzaddi, whose sign signifies a fishhook. The letter Tzaddi is based upon the serpent, symbol of the Tempter.

In esoteric geometry, the symbol is that of a parabola which almost ends in a straight line. One can also use the symbol of four hexagons side by side.

In numerology, we have 6 + 6 + 6 = 18, which is the knock or call-sign given in many Black Lodges, or the "number of the Beast."

In exoteric astrology, this card is attuned with the moon and especially under its aspect of Hecate. Owls and worms are favored by the lunar light of certain phases of the moon. In esoteric astrology, this card is associated with Saturn, but in this case, the neophyte will be accepted by a stern judge. The analogy of the Abyss between the seven sephiroth is the creation of the Supernal Triad.

In magical applications, the name of this arcana is "the Master of Marshes," or "the Ebb, the Flood, and the Salt Sea." The color for rituals is ultra violet. The magical implement is the concave mirror. The incense is ambergris and camphor. The animal is the wolf, and the crayfish. The plant is white poppy.

PRACTICAL DIVINATION:

Upright: The true meaning of this card is temptation, ordeal, collapse. Also, illusion, a depraved imagination, false friends, doubt.

Unfavorable or reversed: This is the card of the traitor or someone who is a slave to black magic. Also, suspicions and superstitions.

XIX THE SUN
The Resplendent Light

SYMBOL: a dot in a circle
HEBREW LETTER: ק QOPH

 This card shows us two children, a girl and a boy, standing in a garden surrounded by a wooden fence. They reach a hand out to each other as well as holding the terminals of a lyre of the Great Work that brings harmony to all. They stand in the middle of a circle of herbs and flowers, with a rose tree on either side. The children indicate the two polarities—the boy symbolizes Reason and the girl Emotion. The rays of the Sun of Truth, the Resplendent Light, the Cosmic Energy beam down. From this radiant sun, twelve rays beam out with the power of the philosophic gold of the alchemists.

INITIATORY SIGNIFICANCE:

This card shows us transmutation, the basis of all Hermetic work when base metal turns into gold. We know today that, because of the loss or augmentation of electrons in an atom, that the atom itself becomes a different thing; so that in losing its electrons, an atom of uranium becomes an atom of lead. The alchemical principle is exactly like this. Physical alchemy is but a veil hiding the true work of spiritual alchemy, where material desires are turned into spiritual ones, and where soul is enriched rather than material life. Alchemy is never successful if there is any sadness in the heart or any doubt in one's thoughts.

SYMBOLIC CORRESPONDENCES:

This card is attuned with the nineteeth letter of the Hebrew alphabet, Qoph, which the Sepher Yetzirah speaks of as a letter that is full of joy.

In esoteric geometry, the symbol of this arcana is the number ten in the middle of nine concentric spheres.

In numerology, 10 + 9 give us the beginning of a cycle. The Initiate in the Mysteries of Osiris carries a chain of 19 scarabs that is associated with the metonic cycle of the moon, which takes 19 years to come round to the same point in the sky. The Sun and the 2 children form a trinity of forms that make up the 19, from adding together the 16 rays with the 2 children and the Sun.

In exoteric astrology, the nineteenth arcana is in rapport with the Sun, which reveals the soul or the individuality. In esoteric astrology, this card is attuned with the sign of Pisces, the sign of the two polarities, and the most powerful for the transmutation of the physical and spiritual character. In magical operations, the name of this arcana is "the Master of the Fire of Worlds," or "the Central Fire of our solar system." The magical instrument is scrying glass. The incense is oblibanum and cinnamon. The animal is the lion, and the plant is the sunflower.

PRACTICAL DIVINATION:

Upright: The true meaning of this arcana is spiritual transmutation. Also, spiritual strength, greatness of soul, courage, spirit, honorable love, restoration of health.

Unfavorable or Reversed: A neglected opportunity, duties abandoned, and decline of energy. Also, lack of success, burnout, overexposure.

XX THE LAST JUDGEMENT
The Resurrection

SYMBOL: an X with a vertical stroke through it

HEBREW LETTER: ר RESH

 This depiction stems from the Middle Ages, following the medieval idea of the Last Judgement. The greater part of the sky is occupied by the head and shoulders of an angel, holding a long trumpet. Attached to this trumpet is a small flag bearing the equal-armed cross. A man and a woman are standing on either side of a child in an attitude of adoration; they have all arisen from their tombs. But our study is the Alchemical Great Work, not Christian theology, so we should not conflate these two lines of symbolism.

INITIATORY SIGNIFICANCE:

All initiatory rites have a symbolic death and a resurrection as a central part of their teaching, as we see in the rites of Eleusis whose followers were instructed in the route of the world beyond. Resurrection is a transmutation, a new birth, a baptism from the water and the heavens, enabling us to step into the life beyond death. The nineteenth arcana shows the transmutation of matter into spirit, while the twentieth arcana shows us the transmutation of the material life into spiritual life—in effect, the spiritualization of all that exists. It is not just that the initiate thinks differently from the non-initiate, but that he is actually in a different state of being, much as a vapor that rises up is not the same thing as water that falls down.

SYMBOLIC CORRESPONDENCES:

The eighth arcana (Justice) corresponds to the eighth letter of the Hebrew alphabet: Resh is a double letter that contains "two truths between Creation and Destruction," which is to say the double gate of death and life.

In esoteric geometry, this arcana is represented by four spheres or circles: earth, water, fire, and air, each having five small flames within them.

In numerology, the number twenty indicates both polarity and unity, and its transmutations show up in the two mirroring calculations of 5 x 4 and 4 x 5. The figure 20 also stands for the two Pillars of Strength and Mercy on the Tree of the Knowledge of Good and Evil, while the Central Pillar carries the figure 12.

In exoteric astrology, it is associated with Jupiter, or more exactly with Zeus. In esoteric astrology, the attribution is to Saturn, if we recall that the sphere of Jupiter is found upon the Pillar of Mercy at Chesed and that of Saturn on the Pillar of Strength, at Geburah.

In magical operations, the name of this arcana is "the Spirit of Primordial Fire," the second alchemical transmutation. The magical object is the visible and invisible lamp. The incense is red sandalwood with ginseng. The animal ascribed to it is the lioness, while the plant is the white dead-nettle.

PRACTICAL DIVINATION:

Upright: The true meaning of this arcana is the spiritualization of matter, "the living gate of the dead." Also, rebirth, liberation, healing, change, ordeal.

Unfavorable or reversed: A lost cause, loss, despair, and retreat. Also, unavoidable scrutiny or examination, postponement.

XXI THE FOOL
The Mystic Fool

SYMBOL the circle:
HEBREW LETTER: ש SHIN

 Medieval versions of the Fool present him in the form of a man clad in a heraldic doublet that is tattered and torn. The little bells of the fool or clown hang from his collar. He carries a beggar's bag on a stick over his shoulder. His tights are torn and a dog is biting at his legs. In front of him is a declivity, wherein a crocodile waits with open jaws.

INITIATORY SIGNIFICANCE:

The central tenet of the major arcana's teaching is about the preparatory ordeals of initiation. But the most difficult thing for the candidate is to give a good account of what he or she understands by that word: for it confers the power to distinguish between the eternal and the temporal, the truth of illusion. Whoever asks for initiation without having acquired the right or the necessary knowledge merely prepares themselves ready for a fall. Following the teaching of the Kabbalah, the candidate tries to harness him- or herself to the divine intelligence in order to become receptive so that the spiritual current might descend upon him or her. Initiation changes the inner character from spiritual agitation to spiritual tranquility, from doubt to confidence; this was also known, in alchemical parlance, as "the transmutation of the Dragon."

SYMBOLIC CORRESPONDENCES:

Shin is the twenty-first letter of the Hebrew alphabet associated with this card: Shin is the messianic letter that governs the head of Adam Kadmon, the Cosmic Man, and that corresponds to the Divine Spark. For Qabalists, there is a direct rapport between Shin, Shaddai, and the arcana of the Fool.

In esoteric geometry, we see the form of a lozenge, with right-angled lines joining the four angles and forming the base of a cross. The horizontal line serves as the base of two isosceles triangles, one above, one below. The vertical line is marking the apex of the higher isosceles triangles, but not the lower one.

In numerology, it is impossible to ignore the following sequence $1 + 2 + 3 + 4 + 5 + 6 = 21$. XXI is the Number of All, and also the Lost Number; it is equally the "the transmutation of the quarternary into the quintessence," according to the arithmetic of the Rosicrucians.

In exoteric astrology, the Fool is associated with the earth; in esoteric astrology, the association is with Fire.

In magical operations, the magical name of the Fool is "the Genius of Transformation." The magical implement is the pilgrim's staff. The incense is olibanum of Java with dried laurel leaves. The creature is the crocodile; the plants are saxifrage and the Passiflora.

PRACTICAL DIVINATION:

Upright: Initiatory powers, denial of the world. Also, innocence, spontaneity.

Unfavorable or reversed: Pride, an antagonism to spiritual things. Also, lack of commitment, heedless action, recklessness.

XXII THE WORLD
The Crown *of* Magicians

SYMBOL a swastika:

HEBREW LETTER: ת TAU

 This arcana is represented by a figure, usually that of a lightly veiled woman, at the middle of a mandorla or oval. The woman dances with great vitality, indicating both the idea of stasis and the rotary movement of the earth on its axis. The mandorla in which she dances is made of a garland of flowers and leaves, with the Four Living Creatures around the Throne in each of the four corners of the card. The Four Creatures of the Apocalypse or the Hayyoth ha Kadosh constitute the fixed cross of the Zodiac, and also as the four Royal Stars of the four Evangelists.

INITIATORY SIGNIFICANCE:

This last card of the major arcana shows eternal activity and eternal rest; the absolute and the relative, the four powers, and the four states of perception. It throws light upon the Philosopher's Stone, the Rosa Mystica, and the Holy Grail. The alchemist affects the World by the accomplishment of the Great Work: the transmutation of matter into spirit; and whoever reaches arcana XXII understands the transmutation of the spiritual into the divine. This card leads the initiate into the presence of God, the Shekinah, to the vision of splendor, the robe of glory and the high places of understanding. Whoever fully understands this arcana will have passed through the twenty-one modes of manifestation and will be ready for the return to the center.

SYMBOLIC CORRESPONDENCES:

The card is associated with the twenty-second Hebrew letter Tau, a priestly number that explains creation through the beauty of movement.

It reveals the mysteries of two numerations: both 21 and 22. Twenty-one is one of the arithmetical representations of the end, being 7 x 3 = 21, while 22 brings us 7 x 3.1314927 or Pi, that attunes the diameter of a circle with its circumference. In esoteric geometry, this card is symbolized by the Yin-Yang, which is described fully on p. 49. There also exists a complex symbol of 21 circles interconnecting with each other in the center of a circle.

In esoteric astrology, it is associated with the Sun, the centripetal force, and with Jupiter, which governs the sephira of Chesed on the Tree of Life, as well as the first emanation beneath the Abyss. In exoteric astrology, it is associated with Neptune.

In magical applications, the name of this card is "the Lord of the Night of Time." The color for rituals is indigo. The perfume and incense is olibanum with Balm of Gilead. The magical implement is the sickle. The animal is the Bull Sphinx.

PRACTICAL DIVINATION

Upright: Ending, completion, universal values, making something available to your community, finalization, sharing resources, working together.

Unfavorable or reversed: Perfectionism, boasting and exaggerating to appear more persuasive, someone who feels the world owes them a living.

CHAPTER 2

THE FOUR TEMPLES OF THE MINOR ARCANA

The Tarot Medieval Minor Arcana

Rolt-Wheeler's model for Tarot Médiéval is largely drawn from the work of Éliphas Lévi, like all Tarots of the Oswald Wirth school (see p. 160). In the entry to King of Scepters, the author remarks that the card immediately follows XXII the World is "card 23." But Rolt-Wheeler did not follow the sequential minor arcana numeration from King to Ace, as used by Lévi, following Etteilla's numbering of all 78 cards in his Tarots from 1 to 78. In Tarot Médiéval, the sequence of Ace to King in each suit has been followed for easier use.

Rolt-Wheeler saw the cards of the four suits as forming four temples. Following a magical association of the suits with the elements, he assigned the following associations to them:

Elements	Tarot Suits	Playing Cards Psychological Functions	Soul Bodies
Air:	Scepters	Clubs Intuition	Spiritual Body
Fire:	Swords	Spades Thought	Mental Body
Water:	Cups	Hearts Emotion	Astral Body
Earth:	Shekels	Diamonds Sensuality	Physical and Etheric Bodies

Anyone familiar with the normal elemental associations in magic and Tarot today will recognize that Rolt-Wheeler has switched over Swords/air and Scepters/fire, with Swords now associated with fire, and Scepters with air. This ascription was often employed in earlier twentieth-century magical thought; it is how the suits appear in Charles Williams's magical Tarot novel of 1932, *The Greater Trumps*.

THE FOUR SUITS

The four suits of the temples are pip cards, numbered from 1 to 10, with only their primary emblems shown in different arrangements, which is how Tarots customarily were made from the fifteenth century to the early twentieth century. The suits are color-coded with blue for Scepters, red for Swords, green for Cups, and brown for Shekels.

SCEPTERS: The wand or baton cards are called Scepters in Tarot Médiéval, representing the scepter of the sovereign or the commander's baton in battle. It is a suit of air, and of intuition.

SWORDS: The sword cards show a long knight's sword, rather than the short cutlass-like sword of the playing-card suit of Spades. It is a suit of fire and thought.

CUPS: The cup cards represent both the Holy Grail and the eucharistic cup of communion. It is a suit of water and emotion.

SHEKELS: The coin suit is anachronistically called Shekels in Tarot Médiéval; these represent the coin offered in the Temple of Jerusalem to purchase the sacrifice or offering. But since the Second Temple in Jerusalem was destroyed in 70 CE, Rolt-Wheeler also speaks more cogently of "Peter's Pence," the tithe offering that Christians made toward the support of the pope. Shekels is a suit of earth and sensuality. Shekels as a title for coins was first introduced into Tarot by Paul Christian.[6]

THE COURT CARDS OF THE FOUR TEMPLES

The sixteen court cards of the four temples in Tarot Médiéval are presented in accordance with the originators' idea of the Middle Ages. The Pages, Knights, and Kings are all presented as male, with only the Queen as female. The Scepter court reveal a Page who goes forth as a messenger, a Knight whose blunt honor defends the loving Queen and the King's domain. The Cup court show the search for the Grail, with the Page bringing the vessel as an acolyte, the Knight as the quester, the Queen as an embodiment of the Grail, while the elderly King is like the Wounded King.

The Sword court deal with the challenging things: the Page attempts to release prisoners from a dank dungeon, the Knight holds truth as his bond, the Queen defends her own castle, while the King is hasty in his decisions. The Shekel court present us with a Byzantine King and Queen, with a Knight who guards their treasure, and a Page who is literally shackled to money or poverty.

THE PAGES

Rolt-Wheeler writes this about the Pages:

"In Tarot Médiéval, the Pages are called Valets in some other places, and sometimes, in the Oswald Wirth system, Slaves or Serfs. In French playing cards, the Valet corresponds to the card we call the Jack in English playing card parlance." As Rolt-Wheeler says, "The word 'valet' possesses the disadvantage of being used for a personal servant, which is not all the character of the Pages of the four temples. The word 'servant' also indicates, in its highest sense, the servant of God. The word 'slave' is one of the much older names of this arcana, but the word has also changed its meaning, and we do not any longer speak of 'the Slave to Beauty' or 'the Slave of the Light.'"

To modern Tarot users, the thought of a Page as any kind of Slave seems very alien. This notion arose in the Oswald Wirth system of Tarot and is still in use in the New Revised Art Tarot of Knap Hall, where we see that the Slaves (Pages) of Swords, Cups, and Coins are all physically manacled at wrist or ankle. This idea arises from Éliphas Lévi's Clavicule of Solomon, where he describes the pages as: "Page of Wands—slave of man, Page of Cups—slave of woman, Page of Swords—slave of love, Page of Coins—slave of children or works."[7]

As Rolt-Wheeler writes:

All in all, we have to look to the Pages as neophytes or proto-neophytes who are just stepping out upon the initiatory path. Steeped in matter still, they are beginning to take up the principles of the esoteric path and are in service to it, apprenticed to high magic. The Pages are shown in differing states and conditions: in the four temples of the Tarot Médiéval, the word "Acolyte" is better for the Page of Cups, and the "Valet" for the Page of Shekels. The Page is elevated in the Cups because he carries the Graal; but he is at a lower level in the Shekels because he is chained to a bag of money.[8]

KNIGHTS

Here, Rolt-Wheeler describes the role of the knight:

"The Knight of the Tarot is removed from modern playing-card decks, where we expect to see just the Valet or Jack, and the Queen and King. This arcana has been called variously the Chevalier, the Cavalier, the Warrior, and the Combatant. But the word "knight" is the most resonant within the Tarot series of King, Queen, Knight, and Page. According to an old astrological law, the twelve houses of the horoscope are in correspondence with the ten number cards, while the eleventh House is attuned with the Knight, and the twelfth House with the Page or Valet. These houses also include their opposites: the fifth house of love and the eleventh House for friendship and protection both agree with the Knight, while the sixth and twelfth houses govern, respectively, servants and work, and restriction, for the Pages.

In the Tarot Médiéval, the Knights of the four temples are designed within a circular background, with colors indicating the nature of the knightly work.[9] Each also carries its own emblem.

QUEENS

Here, Rolt-Wheeler speaks of the queens:

"The expressions of the four queens show their character: the Queen of Scepters is etherial and spiritual, the Queen of Swords is sad but resolute, the Queen of Cups is gracious and hospitable, the Queen of Shekels is cold and lofty."[10]

KINGS

Rolt-Wheeler assigns to the Kings the status of "Royal Stars," following the theories of Paul Christian in his Histoire de la Magie, as follows:

King Scepters: Regulus or "Little King" in Leo
King Swords: Sadalmelik, or "Luck of the King" in Aquarius

King Cups: Aldebaran or "The Follower" in Taurus King Shekels: Antares or "Rival to Mars" in Scorpio

The author speaks of how "the faces of the four kings indicate their character: the spiritual King of Scepters has a pale, even emaciated, face; the King of Swords has the look of a determined warrior; the King of Cups, the Priest-King and Initiator, has a benign look; the King of Shekels is hard, villainous, and looks like a tyrant."[11]

UPRIGHT *and* REVERSED

Note that Rolt-Wheeler speaks of the cards as being "favorable or upright," or "unfavorable or reversed." Sometimes, because he is largely following the meanings of Etteilla in his treatment of the minor arcana, he gives us upright but unfavorable meanings, as well as reversed and favorable ones, depending on the original nature of the card. In any reading, a card can betray its upright position, so be prepared to read it as if it were reversed, and vice versa. See p. 186.

THE FOUR TEMPLES OF THE MINOR ARCANA

THE MINOR ARCANA

The major arcana represent the Greater Mysteries, while the minor arcana represent the Lesser Mysteries. The major arcana are solar and allegorical; the minor arcana are lunar and symbolic. No Tarot is complete without its 78 cards.

The minor arcana are divided into four temples or suits. These are Scepters or Wands, Swords, Cups or Chalices, and Shekels or Coins. The four suits in both medieval and modern playing cards are also divided into the following order: Clubs, Spades, Hearts, and Diamonds. In their astrological correspondences, they are allied with triplicities of air, fire, water, and earth, representing the psychological character of intuition, mentality, emotion, and physical and material states.

THE TEMPLE OF SCEPTERS:

REGION OF THE AIR TRIPICITY

This temple is that of Scepters or the royal emblem of the Baton, like a marshal's baton wielded in command: it corresponds to the playing suit of Clubs, or the emblem of the Trinity, and ecclesiastical authority. The suit of Scepters is allied with the zodiacal signs of the triplicity of air—which are assigned to the sign of Libra, and ruler of the seventh house—and the spiritual state of man.

ACE *of* SCEPTERS

We see a budding branch, like the wand guarding the Ark of the Covenant; it has three circles at its tip, representing the three Supernals of the Tree of Life, while its six branches of the six sephiroth and days of the world's creation: Chesed, Geburah, Tiphareth, Netzach, Hod, and Yesod. The ball at the base of the scepter indicates the physical world and the sephira, Malkuth. On its own, this arcana means creation and the origin of all things. In the Tarot Médiéval, it is represented as a symbol appearing in the sky, surrounded by clouds. It is associated with divine authority, and with any civil authority having a divine mandate.

Upright: This arcana means the beginning, the first step, a move, or an estimate. It could be consulted for the choice of a profession. Its meaning touches equally upon personal belief and indirectly upon the family. Also, establishing a line or posterity,

Unfavorable or reversed: On the high planes it signifies an affliction. This arcana means a loss of protection in a querent's destiny. Also, the end of an affair, discouragement, a fault or mistake, but in a manner more psychological than material.

TWO *of* SCEPTERS

The Two of Scepters is in rapport with Aries and is attuned with the eighth and second houses, which govern its number. The symbol of the 2 Scepters shows two scepters beside each other, indicating two authorities on the spiritual plane. It is incorrect to show them in a crossed position.

Upright: The dominant meaning suggests equality on the high planes, but with the threat of disharmony, conscious or unconscious in the reconciling of opposites. Also, the worry of riches and burdensome responsibilities.

Unfavorable or Reversed: It suggests a change of life that overturns the value of things; the rich who become poor because they are unable to adapt, or the poor who become rich and go into a moral decline. Also, a miracle or surprise.

THREE *of* SCEPTERS

The Three of Scepters is associated with the ninth and third houses. The symbol shows three scepters in the form of an equilateral triangle, whose movement is that of involution and evolution.

Upright: The superior meaning is associated with balance and divine manifestation. On a lower level, it is the arcana of communication, transport, and discoveries. It is favorable for business transactions and the expanding of commerce and trade, also for letters, writing, and correspondence.

Unfavorable or reversed: A poorly judged piece of daring, gambling, and inconclusive projects. Also, interruption, cessation, troubles.

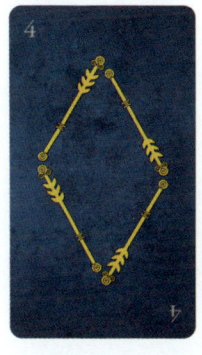

FOUR *of* SCEPTERS

The Four of Scepters is attributed to the tenth and fourth houses. The symbol is shown, not as a square, but rather as a lozenge, in which is the materialization of an ellipse.

Upright: The superior meaning is associated with the harmony of the polarities upon the earthly plane. Also, favorable for all associations, groups, and confraternities. Consolidation, achievement, establishing oneself.

Unfavorable or reversed: It remains favorable but the benefits will be dispersed and scattered, instead of coming toward the one who has won them. Also, insecurity, things tailing off, or coming to an end.

FIVE *of* SCEPTERS

This arcana is drawn like a star of five points or pentagram, with the one point above. It corresponds to the fifth and eleventh houses.

Upright: Its superior meaning is transmutation, also the Sun as "the great magician" of our solar system. Also, riches, gold, money in the bank, your social position, going up in the world, pleasure, and trust among friends.

Unfavorable or reversed: Disagreements among friends, arguments, a tendency to pride. Also, trivial pursuits, contradiction, and being dependent upon the resources of others.

SIX *of* SCEPTERS

This arcana corresponds to the sixth and twelfth houses in astrology. The layout of this card varies in different versions, but here we see the Seal of Solomon, with two triangles superimposed and opposed to each other.

Upright: The dominant meaning of this card is service; whoever obeys may also learn to command. It indicates anyone who serves you or works in a subordinate position, sometimes the messenger, and often domestic quarrels. Also, a friend who supports you.

Unfavorable or reversed: Lack of loyalty or insubordination, and unrewarding work. Also, an unwillingness to serve, checking who you can trust, a faithless friend.

SEVEN *of* SCEPTERS

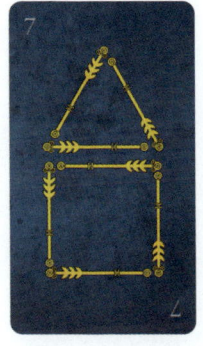

This arcana is associated with the first and seventh houses. The symbol shows a triangle above a square, but it can be shown in a variety of geometric ways in different versions.

Upright: The dominant meaning here is that of harmony or agreement. Meetings, conversations, language, eloquent, or persuasive speech. Also, negotiation, exchange, deliberation, and conference.

Unfavorable or reversed: Duplicity, uncertainty, boastfulness, hurtful words, struggles, and contests. Also, indecision, perplexity, hesitation, vacillation, and the ability to diversify, the versatility of variation.

EIGHT *of* SCEPTERS

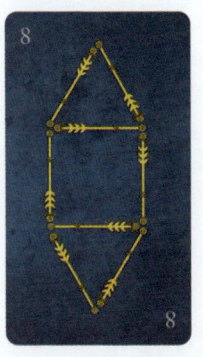

This arcana is associated with the second and eighth houses. The symbol shows two triangles formed of three scepters, one pointing up, the other pointing down, connected by two vertical scepters between them, making a square.

Upright: The superior meaning is that of two currents, one from above and one from below, most often in a disharmonious sense. A betrayal unmasked, the revealing of a secret, surprise, neglect. Also, seeking a place of peace, tranquility, or betterment.

Unfavorable or reversed: Secret meetings, remorse, misunderstanding. Also, overscrupulousness, regret, internal hesitation, uncertainty, the need to transform yourself at a deep level.

NINE *of* SCEPTERS

This card is associated with the third and ninth houses. Six Scepters are arranged as an equilateral triangle pointing upward: inside it three Scepters make a downward-pointing triangle: together they make four equal triangles.

Upright: The chief meaning is that of mystery, or of the unrecognized prophet. It reveals dreams and visions. Also, lack of understanding, boredom, delays, events that slow down, become suspended or feel heavy.

Unfavorable or reversed: Calamity, exile, rumor, and risk. Also, obstacles, disadvantages, adversity. The heaviness of toil, repetitions, and events that thwart your plans.

TEN *of* SCEPTERS

This card is associated with the fourth and tenth houses. The arrangement for this card shows ten Scepters with their handles toward the center and their points toward the outside of a karmic wheel.

Upright: The meaning is karma or destiny. Death, separation, disunity, and emigration. Being overcome by events. Also, hypocrisy, cheating, opposition, conspiracy, or imposture.

Unfavorable or reversed: Betrayal, lies, ruin. Also, fighting a rearguard action, hedged about by obstacles, crushed by events. Dealing with contraries and paradoxes. Being aware of stumbling blocks.

PAGE *of* SCEPTERS

The Page of Scepters is of noble birth, but he has to become accustomed to the most modest kind of work; he is preparing to become a knight, not merely a warrior, but also as a gentleman. As a page he has to be, simultaneously, a servant, confidant, friend, messenger, and squire. In Tarot Médiéval, the Page of Scepters is a young man with a serious face who walks quickly over the silvery and mysterious earth, carrying in his left hand a scroll of parchment—a letter or a proclamation. Despite his youth, the Page gives the impression of being an apostle, or a messenger of inspirational news, who is conscious of his mission. In his right hand he holds a staff topped with a trefoil.

He is attuned to the third house, the house of Intelligence, in astrology, this house rules over travel, mail, messages, newspapers, announcements, etc., which are justly in accord with the given task of the Page of Scepters. He is also in rapport with Gemini, the regnant sign of Mercury on the lower plans, and by Hermes on the superior plane. His connections with the twelfth house indicate esoteric ritual.

Upright: The chief meaning is that of a messenger or a spiritual message, a subordinate or a close relative who is still a youth. Also, a message, letter, news, or advice—with the stress upon the messenger or the way the message is received, not about its content.

Unfavorable or reversed: Traditionally, bad news, losses, even ruin. This may be too categorical for the arcana of air, and it will be more truthful to consider this card as an indicator of indecision, hesitancy, contradictory news, or a lack of practical motivation at a time of necessity.

KNIGHT *of* SCEPTERS

The horse of the Knight of Scepters is galloping hard, giving the impression of a fierce wind whose breath permeates the whole world. The speed and ideal force are found in the movement of this knight. On his shield, and in his right hand, as on the card itself, we see the image of the Scepter portrayed as a six branched stem with a flower of three petals: the stem represents the six sephiroth of Chesed, Geburah, Tiphareth, Netzach, Hod, and Yesod, with the seventh sephira Malkuth at its base, while the flower itself represents the Three Supernals of Kether, Chokmah, and Binah.

The superior meaning of this arcana is the need for activity upon higher planes, for ourselves, for those we love or for our friends. The Knight's haste suggests the speedy passage of time, and the need to seize every occasion to do good. The Knight of Scepters is attuned with the eleventh house, which is governed by Libra, the sign of air, which orders us to choose the desires that raise us up and nourish those ambitions that refine us. It is clear that these desires and ambitions cannot be simply material, because the Knight of Scepters, belonging to the Temple of Scepters, acts upon the ideal plane.

This arcana indicates deployed action, not merely latent power. For this reason, it is a card of great changes, especially in regard to other people. In a question of a new business or commercial association, the Knight of Scepters is not always accepted as a wonderful augury because in a very material transaction, Pegasus, his winged horse cannot be treated like a beast of burden or a draught animal. When divining about a question of new friends, it is necessary to carefully consider if the friends will agree with the character of the Knight of Scepters, because he is always ready to take up his lance in the face of insult: for him, anything suggesting a base action or of an overtly material nature could be an affront.

Upright: In a consultation on a material question, the Knight of Scepters is not always a favorable sign because the querent is going to have an outlook that is not shared with his associates. If these desires or ambitions are self-centered, a falling out is certain. Argumentative, idealist.

Unfavorable or reversed: This arcana is a very bad sign as, on the highest planes, it is an indication of wild impulses, of quixotic projects, of unforeseen aggression, and unjustifiable foundations for misunderstanding. Also, this card means outrageous hopes, vain struggles, and plans that are outside the querent's ability to bring to a good end.

QUEEN *of* SCEPTERS

According to the high tradition, the King and Queen share the governance of the cardinal sign and of the apex of the triangle of their triplicity. The Queen of Scepters is standing; in her right hand is a Scepter, like that of the King, but she is young and gracious, and she steps forward with a light step within a land of dream. The spirituality of the King is acquired by a worthy acceptance of heavy trials, but those of the Queen of Scepters are more integrated with nature. The Queen of Scepters represents platonic love, but few writers exactly render what Plato actually meant by that. In Plato's *Symposium*, Aristophanes speaks of love thus: "The soul of each lover thirsts for something which cannot be described, divining and tracing the footsteps of its obscure desire. If Vulcan should say to these two souls, "My children, do you not desire the closest union and harmony so that you may never be divided by night or day? If so, then I will join your souls, so that you may be one within the other. Is that truly your desire? Will you be happy if I do that? We all know that any worthy person would accept this offer, asking to be intimately mixed together harmoniously with their other, so that the two souls could be as one." This interior harmony is the true meaning of "platonic love."[12] The Queen of Scepters is associated with inspiration, music, the arts, and with the voice of one's own conscience. She indicates "the Holy Spirit within us."

Upright: The chief meaning of this card is of an honorable woman, the mistress of a spotless house, sometimes brusque and authoritarian, she expects to be obeyed. If the question is a material one, she indicates stability, albeit of a rustic sort. The consultant will receive good advice, perhaps given in a frustrating way, but advice that should be heeded. If the consultant is a man, this card is favorable for marriage. It is a bad omen for any deceptions, plots, or conspiracies, because this is a card of total honesty.

Unfavorable or reversed: A tendency to listen to bad advice, to launch shaky projects, to have too much confidence in opportunism, an unwillingness to act according to the best side of your character, believing that a lie will be a support. Also, obstacles, resistance, opposition.

KING *of* SCEPTERS

The King of Scepters is the first of the minor arcana, following directly from the majors. Its sequential number would be 23. This card is associated with the zodiacal sign of Libra, and the seventh house of the horoscope. We see a crowned king, seated upon a throne, carrying in his left hand a scepter symbolizing the wand of office and the trefoil of the suit of Clubs. He is elderly, and his face is that of an ascetic.

The chief meaning of this arcana is spiritual sovereignty, or the high planes of the intellectual that can become intuitive. In the highest kind of divination, the King of Scepters is favorable for all questions concerning spiritual self-control, and all ideal ambitions. This arcana is equally favorable for partnership, especially with an older person or more experienced one.

Students of Tarot must be warned that some mistaken understandings of the word "wand" assign this whole Temple of Scepters to a material level. Always in divination there is a tendency where it is useful to cling to the most material of meanings, but we must not lose sight of the superior meanings.

According to traditional divination, this arcana represents the Father, not solely as the Master or Sage in his teaching, or the king on his throne, but also the responsible father of a family. Anciently this card was interpreted as the lord of a domain, a noble countryman, or the farmer of an estate. The nobility of work is accorded to even the simplest laborer, but the dignity of work is lost when employees are abused.

Upright: This card indicates honesty, albeit of a rustic or unsophisticated kind. Tricks do not always succeed, or cannot be sustained for long, but honesty, perseverance, and personal, continual work remain the true road to success. An idler becomes a parasite, but that is the limit of his powers. If the consultant is a woman and the question is about marriage or relationship, the response is favorable.

Unfavorable or reversed: Rough or severe justice, a father who is too hard on his children. Also, in unfavorable combinations, it indicates that probity and honesty are tainted, or that the consultant is trying to convince himself of his own judgement.

THE TEMPLE *of* SWORDS

REGION OF THE FIRE TRIPICITY

This temple is that of the Swords or the Spades suit. The Sword suggests that which was held by the Seraphim guarding the entrance to the Earthly Paradise after the Fall. The Sword is a symbol of the knight, to whom duty is most important, for the protection of the weak and the help of those in distress. The emblem of the playing-card suit of Spades is that of the cutlass or short sword of ancient times, while in Tarot Médiéval, the blade is longer. We note the English word "spade" derives from the word "spada" or "sword" from medieval Italian and has nothing to do with digging! The Swords are associated with the triplicity of fire of Aries, Leo, and Sagittarius and the mental state of man.

ACE *of* SWORDS

We see a Sword with its tip upright; the blade terminates in three curves. As a symbol of chivalry, the Ace of Sword is more usually represented as a rapier, with a crown over its point. This sword represents honor, not fighting.

Upright: This arcana means protection, but can also become the Sword of Vengeance. Passion, excess, and the will to action; authority, endurance, and justice. Also, going to extremes, deep engagement with things.

Unfavorable or reversed: According to the nature of the querent's question, this can indicate punishment, or the use of brutal and violent methods. Winnings or money with this arcana reversed are never lasting. Also, pregnancy, conception, and fecundity.

TWO *of* SWORDS

The Two of Swords is attuned to the second house and with Aries. The card shows two swords in their sheaths, standing beside each other. The symbolism of crossed swords is an incorrect one, since the character of this card is rather one of mutual assistance.

Upright: The superior meaning of this arcana is mutual association and assistance, professional friendship. This card does not have the sentimental partnership of the 2 of Cups nor the business associations of the 2 of Shekels, but rather signifies friendship, brotherhood, political support, affinity, and helping the weak.

Unfavorable or reversed: Help refused, family opposition, and a person unworthy of friendship, a lack of tact. Bad faith, deception, falsity, and calculated deceit. Superficial engagement or without commitment.

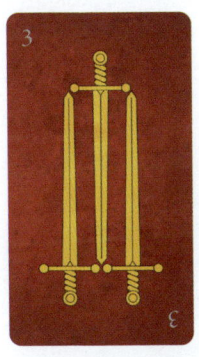

THREE *of* SWORDS

The card shows a central sword point downward, and two opposing swords facing upward. It is associated with the third house.

Upright: The superior meaning suggests a lack of foresight and destiny's opposition to the fulfilment of your wishes and hopes. Also, a separation, a leave-taking, bad news, unlucky, interruption to plans, distance, aversion, separation, and division.

Unfavorable or reversed: A scandal, a break in one's habits or daily routines, exile or a solitary life. Confusion, dementia, distraction, miscalculation, loss, dispersion. Also, loss, mistakes, derailed, or delayed.

FOUR *of* SWORDS

This arcana is associated with the fourth house. The Four of Swords is arranged in a manner whereby their pommels form a parallelogram, and their crossed points form a square. Two crossed swords above, and two below.

Upright: The dominant meaning touches upon all kinds of solitude or meditation, quietness, ease after sorrow. Also, carefulness, wise behavior, and foresight, as well as sympathy, prudence, and retreat.

Unfavorable or reversed: Neglect, abandonment, giving up on things, withdrawal from daily life or usual affairs. Taking necessary precautions, good economy, and judicious reserve. Also, harmony, music, moderation.

FIVE *of* SWORDS

The five takes on the character of black magic as its shape is the inverted pentagram. Generally speaking, the Swords take the form of daggers: a very sinister sign.

Upright: The dominant meaning is a black transmutation, where ordinary matters devolve to your detriment. This can be a tragic intervention, a state of agony, a sense of isolation, a series of challenges. Also, active menace, a scandal, dishonor, ruin.

Unfavorable or reversed: Widowhood, a burial, a funeral, living with loss, mourning. Grief, affection, disappointment, and retirement. Also, prejudice, marked out or set aside.

SIX *of* SWORDS

The Six of Swords is exclusively attuned to the sixth house. The design shows the swords seeking to be in equilibrium, three swords with hilts facing up above, and three swords with hilts facing down below. Crossed swords is mistaken.

Upright: The superior meaning is the balancing of the spiritual with the material. In divination, this card shows itself as a way or means, a road or approach, a feeling, an unknown end, a message or news. Also, a course, example, or staged program of education.

Unfavorable or reversed: Denunciation, unveiling, a discovery that something is wrong or a confession. Also, a declaration, charter, constitution, or census, as well as a discovery, research, or vision that clarifies the unknown.

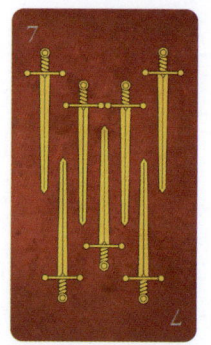

SEVEN *of* SWORDS

The Seven of Swords is associated with the seventh house. The swords are shown standing perpendicularly, three above with points downward, and four below with points facing upward.

Upright: The dominant meaning is a black transmutation, where ordinary matters devolve to your detriment. This can be a tragic intervention, a state of agony, a sense of isolation, a series of challenges. Also, active menace, a scandal, dishonor, ruin.

Unfavorable or reversed: Widowhood, a burial, a funeral, living with loss, mourning. Grief, affection, disappointment, and retirement. Also, prejudice, marked out or set aside.

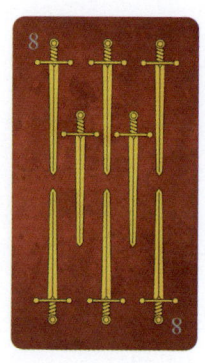

EIGHT *of* SWORDS

This arcana is associated exclusively with the eighth house. The swords are shown in 3 lines made up of two pairs of swords with points meeting, with two single swords pointing upward in between the three lines.

Upright: The superior meaning is the balancing of the spiritual with the material. In divination, this card shows itself as a way or means, a road or approach, a feeling, an unknown end, a message or news. Also, a course, example, or staged program of education.
Unfavorable or reversed: Denunciation, unveiling, a discovery

that something is wrong or a confession. Also, a declaration, charter, constitution, or census, as well as a discovery, research, or vision that clarifies the unknown.

NINE *of* SWORDS

This arcana is exclusively in rapport with the ninth house. The symbolism shows a great sword around which are displayed eight smaller swords: four above and four below, pointed toward the center of the larger sword in paired chevrons.

Upright: The superior meaning is one of the last stages of initiation. A cleric or ecclesiastical matters, religion, ceremony, ritual. Also, nightmares or warning dreams, devotion.

Unfavorable or reversed: Blasphemy, moral laxity, haunted by omens and signs. Justified distrust, fears, and conjectures that manifest, doubts that linger.

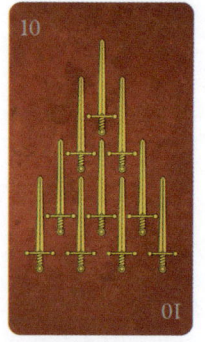

TEN *of* SWORDS

This card is associated with the tenth house. It is shows a triangle of ten swords with their points downward, four at the top, three below them, then two, and lastly a single sword below, which best expresses the heaviness of this card.

Upright: The chief meaning is spiritual protection or extreme punishment. It is for this reason that the interpretation is often affliction and sometimes elevation. Distress, tears, bankruptcy. Also, pain and sadness.

Unfavorable or reversed: Losses turn to gain, death in a state of grace, a gracious ending, retirement after long achievement. Also, advantage, the grace to change things, and usurpation.

PAGE *of* SWORDS

The Page of Swords resonates with the sign of Sagittarius and the ninth house. The Page of Swords is shown as a young man, in coat of mail, with a red tunic. He advances into the darkness of a cavern, a torch upheld in his left hand, and a drawn sword in his right. Before him is a skull; several bones from a skeleton are seen in the darkness. He advances slowly, but without doubt; the ambiance suggests the dungeons of a fortress taken by assault, where prisoners are aware of their release at the hands of the Page.

This card is about subjective thought led to objectivity. This can be applied to the reformer, to the missionary, to the liberator. There is a spiritual energy here, but an understanding of the necessity of fighting against ignorance and shadows. It is good that there should be such bravery, for prudence is a necessary attribute in great mental adventures of the spiritual realm.

Upright: We see here the optimism, enthusiasm, personal valor, and endurance. These meanings show us the explorer, the pioneer, the traveller, the observer, the go-between. A test, a plan. A prophet, a preacher, a learned person, and someone who is willing to experiment and try things out.

Unfavorable or reversed: A traitor or spy. A profane or impious person. A criminal. Pride, having too much self-confidence. Daring to do evil, risking the safety of others. Also, the ability to speak or compose spontaneously

KNIGHT *of* SWORDS

The Knight of Swords is associated with the fifth house. In Tarot Médiéval, the Knight of Swords is drawn on a galloping horse, but a gallop that is well controlled by the reins of the knight. The horse is completely under the domination of the one who rides it. Self-control cannot prevent enthusiasm. Even more than the King, the Knight of Swords should be a true knight, reverential toward his God, loyal to his king, worthy of his country, faithful to his love, just, proud, courageous, without fear or reproach. In the mental realm, and especially on the highest planes, he must know how to discern or to find the right and truth. He must speak openly and frankly, he must support the good so that he can help the oppressed, and he must act by himself, having the courage of his convictions, and without depending upon a brotherhood or a group. He must struggle for what is just and honorable at all costs; he must be the enemy opposed to trickery, to lies, and to corruption.

It is important that he is ready to act masterfully or under instruction, because the tripicity of fire is in mental rapport and, if goodness is his guide, he may help others without false pride or presumptuous aims. We do not ask him for subtlety and diplomacy, but honor, courage, and zeal. The meanings very much mirror the spirit of the Middle Ages, where the duelist or bravo is mixed up with the soldier.

Upright: Among the true meanings, we can include anyone of the military profession, a warrior, soldier, or even a bandit. War, duel, brawl, or dispute. Wound or accident. Courage, skill, enthusiasm, violence. Opposition, resistance, defence. Also, a spy or investigator.

Unfavorable or reversed: A violent character, bestial or stupid. Clumsy and oafish, a man of the ranks, or at the heart of the gang. A zealot or fanatic. Extravagance, vanity, stupidity. A hidden assassin, rapacity, and cowardice. A vigilante. Also, the unexpected, and the ability to speak spontaneously without preparation.

QUEEN *of* SWORDS

The King and Queen are both under the cardinal sign of their associated triplicity, of fire, the sign of the Ram, and the first house. Normally, both authority and the legal decision-making belong to the masculine polarity, but when circumstances force a woman to be the master, she can be harder, more severe, and often crueler than a man. On the Tree of Knowledge of the Good and Evil, the feminine pillar is one of Severity, while the masculine pillar is that of Mercy. The association of mercy with just the feminine polarity is mistaken.

In Tarot Médiéval, we find the expression of this authority forced upon a woman by taxing circumstances. A sorrowful queen in coat of mail stands upon the ramparts of her castle. She carries her shield and unsheathed sword. She is the chatelaine, a widow, or forced to defend her castle against invaders else her husband is in far-away lands. The mental triplicity to which she belongs indicates that the woman is ready to defend her household, if it is in danger, and she will develop her courage, intuition with a firm will and often, that she is the true inspiration for victory. When a woman works in the mental realm of creative thought, idealism, and enthusiasm, she can achieve much. If she does not follow an artistic vocation herself, then inspiration is her special gift where, in periods of difficulty and depression, feminine firmness and endurance is the best support of her family.

Upright: When the consultation is for a man, this arcana indicates dangers arising from jealousy or the hate of a woman, probably for very justifiable reasons. For a female consultant, it can reveal desertion, separation, abandonment, making it a necessity for her to make her life by her own means or by her own courage. In a general way, it can indicate widowhood, divorce, infertility, or conjugal negligence.

Unfavorable or reversed: For a man—the revenge of a woman, often motivated by insult; for a woman—the malice of other women, with grave consequences. Bigotry, hypocrisy, and bad advice are also part of this arcana's picture. Also, the ability to work with finesse, bigotry, and hypocrisy.

KING *of* SWORDS

The Temple of Swords is attuned with the fire triplicity in both an astrological and a psychological sense, with the mind. The King of Swords is the dominant card of the four figures in the Temple of Swords, under the governance of the sign of the Ram and of the first house of the horoscope. In Tarot Médiéval, the symbolism shows a king, crowned with a steel helmet, in a coat of mail, holding a sword in his right hand, and a scepter in his left hand. He is seated upon a simple throne. Just as all the people of the Scepters temple are drawn in an etherial blue, so all the Temple of Swords court are drawn in red, the color of fire. The King governs the sign of the Ram, but also that of the Lion, second of the fire signs, which are embroidered upon his robe, and he is the only king with a pair of spurs, emblem of Sagittarius, the third of the fire signs.

The King of Swords indicates the development of the true personality, consciously developed. He rules the power of decision, the force of will, both fervor and action. He acts more practically than the King of Scepters, and more directly upon world affairs. His decisions are sometimes hasty, unwise, and daring, but even his mistakes lead to a good result.

Upright: For a long time, this arcana has had the meaning of military career or of public office. With the authority of justice, the king is the Supreme Court of Appeal. Rather than the soldier and the lawyer, we should see here the general and the judge. According to some traditions, this arcana represents the principles in a law case. The meaning will be that right itself will be the winner, more so than the consultant. Also, an assessor, professional, doctor, or legal advocate.

Unfavorable or reversed: According to tradition, this arcana reversed shows a man who harms the consultant; in a law case he will indicate an unfavorable judgement. If other cards in the reading are less propitious and especially harmful, we attribute the meaning of evil intentions, maliciousness, cruelty, and criminal activity. Also, criminal actions, cruelty, atrocity, inhumanity.

THE TEMPLE OF CUPS

The Cups or Chalices are attuned to the triplicity of water, made up of Cancer, Scorpio, and Pisces, and with the emotional state of man. Human emotions cover a wide range of expression: pleasure and sadness, pride and humility, service and boastfulness, love and hate, etc. Cups are not restricted to just the material emotions of family affection or carnal love. The Temple of Cups touches upon the more elevated emotions as well. The symbol for the third temple is that of the Chalice or Cup. It is formed of three parts, symbolizing the three planes: the base of the emotions, the stem of the mental plane, and the bowl of the spiritual plane. The bowl of the Cup is circular, the stem is octagonal, and the foot has six sides. Its form is preferable to that of the chalice because this form can be applied to the three planes. To portray it as a goblet or drinking glass is to show ignorance of its superior sense of this temple.

ACE *of* CUPS

In the Tarot Mediéval, the symbolism of the Cup is that of the Chalice of the Holy Grail or the Eucharistic Cup. We have to judge each Cup card from its application to the planes: on the emotional plane, the Ace of Cups signifies the carnal desires between two people; on the mental place, the tenderness of the courts of love, and of mutual inspiration and accord between two souls on the spiritual plan. We see a cup over which the spirit of the Divine Light, the dove of the Holy Spirit, descends to consecrate the wine and the life in the chalice.

Upright: This arcana means abundance, the descent of emotional forces, inspiring and spiritualizing. On a lower level, the interpretation can be a joyous occasion or a pleasant period. Also, devotion, continuance, and constancy.

Unfavorable or reversed: A change, infidelity, tiredness, a misunderstanding, and a false teaching. Also, alteration, variation, diversity, reversion, or translation, metamorphosis.

TWO *of* CUPS

The Temple of Cups is attuned with Cancer and with the fourth and fifth houses. The symbol shows two Cups or Chalices, one beside the other, indicating the two polarities. An old tradition says that the Cups contain the pure and the impure, and that this arcana possesses the meaning of choice.

Upright: The superior meaning is of love, especially celestial love or sublime love. In the upright position, this arcana means an invitation, a meal, a festival, abundance, and faithfulness. Also, an affectionate friendship, attraction, or affinity.

Unfavorable or reversed: An unfavorable change, infidelity, or irritation. Also, longing, lust, desire, sensuality, appetite, passion, or a relationship where one is more dominant.

THREE *of* CUPS

The card shows us three cups arranged in the form of a triangle, one above and two below. It is associated with the sixth and third houses.

Upright: The superior meaning is emotional and spiritual evolution, associated with both intelligence and spirit. Also, success, victory, happiness, love that satisfies, recovery after illness.

Unfavorable or reversed: The sense that a project you wish to achieve is actually illusory, sadness in victory, lack of recognition for your service. Also, speeding to conclude a project, terminating an association.

FOUR *of* CUPS

The Temple of Cups is attuned with Cancer and with the fourth and fifth houses. The symbol shows two Cups or Chalices, one beside the other, indicating the two polarities. An old tradition says that the Cups contain the pure and the impure, and that this arcana possesses the meaning of choice.

Upright: The superior meaning is of love, especially celestial love or sublime love. In the upright position, this arcana means an invitation, a meal, a festival, abundance, and faithfulness. Also, an affectionate friendship, attraction, or affinity.

Unfavorable or reversed: An unfavorable change, infidelity, or irritation. Also, longing, lust, desire, sensuality, appetite, passion, or a relationship where one is more dominant.

FIVE *of* CUPS

This arcana corresponds to the fifth and eighth houses and is plainly attuned with its traditional meanings. The Cups form a lozenge with a cup in the middle, and two cups both above it and below it.

Upright: The dominant meaning is kindness. Marriage for love, and inheritances that will not be gained without annoyance. Also, a donation, grant, or gift that is given or you don't have to work for.

Unfavorable or reversed: Problems with aging parents, the loss of a case concerning an inheritance, difficulty in obtaining money owed to you, kindness thrown in your face. Also, family ties; an acquaintance, rapport, or liaison with someone.

SIX *of* CUPS

This arcana is associated with the sixth and ninth houses. The Cups are arranged in three sets of pairs, creating two lines, indicating the symbolism of a clairvoyant channel.

Upright: The dominant meaning is of clairvoyance, clairaudience, psychism, and spiritualism. The card indicates the past and the future, prediction, happiness arising from the things we have forgotten. Also, history, antiquity, or memory, and the return of something thought long gone or lost.

Unfavorable or reversed: An attempt to restart something that is badly or roughly planned, or that is quickly stifled by laziness, problems arising from presumption or self-assertion. Also, the future, a renewal, a repetition, or reworking.

SEVEN *of* CUPS

This arcana is attuned with the seventh and tenth houses. The card is shown divided by two diagonals, giving us two sets of three cups arranged in a triangle above each other, with two a single cup beneath them.

Upright: The chief meaning is that of mystery, but without a good balance, suggesting curiosity or credulity, rather than faith. It usually indicates doubt and indecision, especially in emotional matters, often led by an exaggerated regard for a loved one.

Unfavorable or reversed: Poor personal judgement, badly placed suspicions, deception, or error lead you astray. Also, an intention, resolution, or willful determination that you wish to bring about.

EIGHT *of* CUPS

This arcana is in rapport with the eighth and twelfth houses. The symbol shows the cups in perfect balance, with three cups above and below, and two between them.

Upright: Judging the material and spiritual balance of a plan, whether something is truly satisfactory or not. If it is found wanting, then backtracking to find the balance point, or abandoning the plan. Also, it can stand as a significator for a young woman who is honorable and modest, as well as consent given.

Unfavorable or reversed: Instability or laziness prevent success. Someone's modesty is really hiding wantonness. Also, a show, spectacle, public event, or celebration.

NINE *of* CUPS

This card is attuned to the ninth and twelfth houses. We see eight cups forming a lozenge with one cup at the center: the nine cups together indicate the heavenly, astral, and physical realms.

Upright: The chief meaning is that of a spiritual or material victory. Philanthropic action, expansive feelings, pleasure, gain, wishes fulfilled. Also, achievement, advantage, celebrating success.

Unfavorable or reversed: A success that leads to a collapse, optimism burns and crashes, self-denial, self-conceit gets in the way. Also, taking your ease, being openhearted and simple, or being too familiar or audacious.

TEN *of* CUPS

This arcana is attuned with the first and tenth houses. The symbol is one of the most powerful of the minor arcana, showing the cups arranged in the form of the ten sephiroth of the Tree of Knowledge of Good and Evil.

Upright: The superior meaning is an elevated morality, clear philosophy. The purchase of a property, a promotion, honors, and awards, being the king of your castle, and lasting happiness. Also, town or country, the family home.

Unfavorable or reversed: Violence, wasteful squandering of resources, a corrupt citizen or official. Also, public or civil violence, revolution, indignation, national agitation.

PAGE *of* CUPS

This arcana is attuned to the Temple of Feelings, and the watery triplicity. We see here more of the servant than the page, someone who has not stepped out of his usual designation, but who attempts a higher stage of initiation. This card is associated with the twelfth house of the horoscope, the house governing rites and ceremonies. This house is classed as one of the three esoteric houses, but is also about falling, imprisonment, and bad luck.

The card shows a young man in a monastic habit who slowly advances carrying a chalice containing the consecrated elements. The chalice is covered, indicating that this is not the right time to unveil the mysteries. Also, it is not himself who is the priest: he is nothing but an acolyte. He is dressed in dark green with a blue hood. The Servant of Cups is he who comes to understand the profundity and beauty of the world of feeling. This young neophyte is astonished by the marvelous knowledge that is unfolding before him; here is a young man who feels within himself for the first time the sense of romance. This stage is always associated with contemplation and silence. Sursum corda—let us lift up our hearts!

Upright: The medieval traditions hide a more serious meaning to the attribution normally given this card of "a fair-headed youth." We uncover the meaning of intellectual work, of scientific study, of reflection. According to another tradition, it is also that of a profession, job, or livelihood. The card also means the meeting with a partner of ethical behavior and good character, often of the opposite sex.

Unfavorable or reversed: The card is regarded as harmful to the consultant, because it suggests an easy flattery, a false affection, a dubious meeting, or hanging out with a bad set of companions. For the consultant, the card suggests that hypocrisy is around. Also, an inclination or tendency to overindulge.

KNIGHT *of* CUPS

This card is associated with Cancer and the fourth house, and with Scorpio and the eighth house, which governs death. In the Tarot Médiéval, the Knight of Cups does not ride in haste or at the charge, like the Knights of Scepters and Swords. With the visor of his helmet lowered, he advances slowly on a white horse. The harnesses of his horse are green, and we see his blazon of a cup upon his shield.

Love and death are rightly associated as we shall see here in the sign of the Scorpion. Love is not imagined as a means of life, as the fifth house designates, but as the basis for a spiritual development leading to survival. A man or a woman is classified immediately and irreparably by their conception of love. A concentration upon carnal matters prevents any emotional elevation or the intimate gentleness of harmonious polarity, and immediately prevents all possibility of spiritual sublimation.

Upright: The traditions see this card as representing a young, handsome, and attractive man, but one who should not be judged simply by his manners or fine words. The card suggests a new loving interest or a connection, but one that is always associated with an opinion, not to be taken as signifying a current or more sexual attraction. A charmer, or inspirer of affection.

Unfavorable or reversed: When reversed, the menace of this card is increased. According to tradition, it reveals deceit, especially the kind where the victim is tricked despite having their eyes open. For the same reason, the seducer often appears fleetingly sincere, but his attentions are motivated by passing enthusiasm rather than any sincere reciprocation. Also, a smooth operator, flexible to and manipulative of emotional circumstances.

QUEEN *of* CUPS

This arcana, along with the King of Cups, belongs with the fourth house of the horoscope, which governs the household and our birth. All initiatory schools accept "the Path of the Vestal," or "the Path of the Hearth-fire," having chastity and love of truth at its heart. It is not only Vesta or Hestia who is the goddess of the household, but she is also the guardian of the integrity of the word and of constancy to one's vows. The presence of a woman is necessary for each vow taken before the tutelary gods of the hearth, and the presence of a vestal has been necessary at the signing of all treaties or agreements of state.

The card shows a young and beauty queen, thoughtful, full of dignity, holding a chalice by its cup, ready to pour it out to whoever is worthy. Here the peace and happiness of the household is revealed; for the woman who brings unhappiness upon the household is a traitor, and she who dishonors the heart works for the Lord of the Dark Countenance. In medieval lore, the sacred mission of women was to give birth to children, if she had not received the task of inspirer or prophetess, in which case, she would bring forth spiritual children in others. In both cases, woman is herself the chalice of the Holy Grail. In an esoteric sense, the power of woman in the fourth house helps the soul to pass through the terrestrial world to teach the lunar and astral worlds.

Upright: The ancient title of this arcana is "a blond woman," also a generous, good, and frank woman. In a reading for a woman, this card indicates honesty and chastity, but not celibacy. If the consultant is a man, and if the question concerns his feelings, then this card is favorable for all well-intentioned emotions. Also, wisdom and honesty.

Unfavorable or reversed: An unworthy woman runs the household, being either dishonest or unfaithful; it also indicates laziness, negligence, or indifference. A household in uproar or without welcome. Also, corruption or scandal afflict the house.

KING *of* CUPS

The Cups are comparable with the Hearts in the playing cards. Like them, the Cups cover a wide range of emotions. The card shows us a crowned king, holding in his right hand a cup and in his left a scepter. The cup is covered with a "corporal" or veil of fine linen because the wine of the chalice is not for all the world. The king's robe is a deep green, symbolic of the generative, protean power of nature. This card is associated with the sign of Cancer and the fourth house of the horoscope: the most mysterious point of which is titled "the Point of Silence at the Center," and "the Gate of the Birth of Men."[13] This house indicates the prenatal period. The breast of the mother is sometimes called "the chalice."

The King is very old, with white hair and beard, his face thin and haggard, holding in his hands the sacred drink that elucidates the mysteries. If the birth of man is a blossoming, it is also a secret. The wine of experience opens the centers, giving onto the subtle bodies, but only through continual discovery. The King of Cups never lowers nor gives to drink of his cup to those who are fueled by basal emotions, or by vulgar or carnal appetites.

Upright: This arcana, in medieval symbolism, always carries the meaning of a powerful blond king and indicates someone of superior status. This card also resonates with the alchemical transmutation of base metal into gold. The kingly sage, in modern parlance, represents an honest man of some gravity. Also, a person of science or art.

Unfavorable or reversed: A man with grandiose airs that are not actually his, someone who pretends to knowledge but does not actually possess it, an imposter and charlatan, who is always looking to advance himself. Also, someone who extorts money through trickery or crime, or someone sunk in corruption or scandal.

THE TEMPLE *of* SHEKELS, COINS, DENIERS, *or* PANTACLES

Following the triplicity of the planes, the Shekels are attuned to the triplicity of earth, of Taurus, Virgo, and Capricorn, the material plane, and to the physical life of man. This is also the suit of questions to do with one's state in life: being a boss and worker, a cleric or lay person. In the Middle Ages, Pantacles, or charms in circular form, once carried a cross: they were carried to maintain health by expelling the spirit of the illness. Coins or Deniers were small change, riches that accumulate, or savings, as in "St. Peter's Pence." The Coins in Tarot Mediéval are Shekels, symbolizing the money used at the Temple of Jerusalem with which to buy offerings.

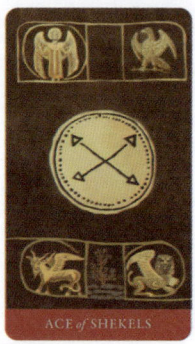

ACE *of* SHEKELS

The central symbol is a golden, circular disk with an unsophisticated design, carrying the Elemental Cross, or Cross of Nature; the Cross of St. Andrew is the cross applied to the human condition. Each terminal of this cross has a triangle pointing outward. In the top left quadrant of the card is a winged angel, in the top right an eagle; in the bottom left quadrant a winged ox, and in the bottom right, a winged lion. The Temple of Shekels is attuned with the earth triplicity, with Capricorn and House 10.

Upright: On the high plane of thought, this arcana means the satisfaction that comes from the doing of one's duty, and the great richness that comes from not giving oneself up to one's desires. On the inferior plane, it means happiness, satisfaction, contentment, healing, and gain. Also, enchantment, marvels, joys, and pleasure, as well as the perfect tincture that brings health.

Unfavorable or reversed: The frittering away of money or crumbling of health, the need to live on your capital, riches that cannot be used, investments that give no returns, and an affair with ruin. Also, your savings or capital, starter finance, and whatever is dear or precious to you.

TWO *of* SHEKELS

The Two of Shekels is in rapport with the second and eleventh houses and with Capricorn. The symbol shows two Shekels, one above the other in equal honor.

Upright: The superior meaning indicates that the obstacles in the material world are very often the means by which we are pushed toward the Spiritual Way. Riches are rarely or never an indication of an occult vocation. It also means confusion, difficulty, obstruction, disputes, strikes, gain with loss.

Unfavorable or reversed: A piece of advice, a danger, an anonymous letter, a denunciation, or a secret. Also, a letter, message, written book, or document.

THREE *of* SHEKELS

Ancient symbolisms give this card three small ladders of three steps each, but in Tarot Médiéval, the three shekels are shown alone, rising from bottom right to top left transversely like the ancient version. It is associated with the twelfth and third houses.

Upright: The superior meaning of this arcana is the danger of a degradation of character through riches. Whatever is great and powerful, generosity and philanthropy. Also, building and creating, something important, noble, or magnificent.

Unfavorable or reversed: Mediocrity, popularity, false glory, pursuit of impossible aims. Also, childishness, frivolous, weakness or faint-heartedness, rejected, lowly, or worthless.

FOUR *of* SHEKELS

This arcana is attuned to the first and fourth house. The shekels are arranged as a parallelogram, with equal angles, two coins above and two below.

Upright: The dominant meaning is understanding differences, and the desire to bring harmony. A gift, an offering, a kindness, reconciliation, taking the initiative, working locally. Also, a tip, donation, or benefit.

Unfavorable or reversed: A questionable gift, a cancellation, being suspicious or overly cautious, envy, prejudice. Also, a limit, boundary, barrier, or obstacle that prevents your plan. Being surrounded, circumscribed, or intercepted.

FIVE *of* SHEKELS

The shekels are arranged in a parallelogram, with the fifth at the center. This arcana is attuned to the second and fifth houses.

Upright: Its dominant meaning is the necessity of uniting the two polarities in all our actions, in order to gain success. Also, a lover, marriage, mutual attraction, determination. Also, to cherish, adore, or find suitable.

Unfavorable or reversed: Bad behavior, a life off the rails, confusion, sensual egotism, poverty, excessive toil, obstinacy. Also, trouble or confusion, damage or deterioration to what is essential to you.

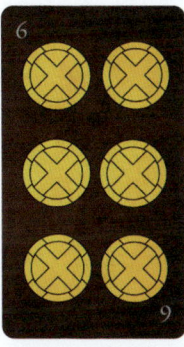

SIX *of* SHEKELS

This arcana is attuned with the sixth and third houses. The shekels are arranged in two columns, like the pillars of Jachin and Boaz in the Temple of Solomon.

Upright: The dominant meaning is of vigilance, immediate action, as well as the dangers of delay, or the squandering of your time. The present, one's present life, prompt decisions, influencing your local community. Also, what is unfolding right now or what is witnessed.

Unfavorable or reversed: Heaviness of spirit, a false direction, losses due to lack of attention, being mean about money, or spendthrift. Also, desire for material possession, zeal, jealousy, and vigilance.

SEVEN *of* SHEKELS

This arcana is attuned with the fourth and seventh houses. In Tarot Médiéval, the shekels are stylized, more like ancient versions of this card that show a bag or net containing seven pieces of gold. Two large coins above and below, with three smaller ones between them.

Upright: The chief meaning of this arcana is of material perfection, victory upon the earthly plane. It usually indicates gold, riches, or money in hand. Cultivating the land, investing in business. Also, the power of the moon to grow and enhance or ebb and shrink whatever grows, depending on its phases.

Unfavorable or reversed: Deception in business, fear, worry, defeat, hopes disappointed, becoming a slave to your business. Also, impatience, personal application, mistrust, and care for your possessions.

EIGHT *of* SHEKELS

This arcana corresponds to the eighth and fifth houses, which govern sexuality and love. The shekels are shown in two groups of four: four smaller coins forming a square in the center, with four larger coins forming as a lozenge around them.

Upright: The chief meaning is "love that overcomes death." An enduring love and moral support. A small amount of money, savings. Also, the significator for a dark young woman.

Unfavorable or reversed: Carnality and disgust, being overscrupulous about detail when the bigger picture is being missed. Also, avarice and usury, loans that fall due, and hoarding.

NINE *of* SHEKELS

This arcana is attuned with the sixth and ninth houses. The design shows one large centrally positioned coin, with four smaller coins both above and below it.

Upright: The chief meaning is patriotism, and the struggle against corruption. Realization of your hopes in the finalization of a project, a business or international trip, an inheritance. Also, accomplishment, fulfilment, and enjoying the effects of your work.

Unfavorable or reversed: An irresponsible citizen, unsocial behavior, greedy but miserly, theft. Also, financial swindling or deception, vain pretensions to live a rich life, projects that fail.

TEN *of* SHEKELS

This card is attuned with the seventh and tenth houses. We see two sets of four smaller coins arranged in a lozenge above and below, while two greater coins stand between them.

Upright: The chief meaning is household, especially a hospitable and joyous one: a house, a castle, or even a thatched cottage. Provision for your old age, material comfort. Also, extended family and ancestors, your nation or people.

Unfavorable or reversed: Debts, mortgages, a temporary shelter, having to leave your home. Also, gambling with your patrimony, fortune-telling, the fate of fortune, gaming, and betting.

PAGE *of* SHEKELS

As stated earlier, the title "Page" is a better name for this figure in the four temples of the Tarot Médiéval, but the word "Acolyte" is better for the Page of Cups, and "Valet" for the Page of Shekels. The Page is elevated in the Cups because he carries the Graal; but he is at a lower level in the Shekels because he is chained to a bag of money. This card is attuned with Mercury and the sixth house of the horoscope.

We see the Page of Shekels in prison, chained by the leg to a great coin on the earth. He is not captive because of poverty, because he is seated upon a chest, not a bench, and a bag of golden coins is open before him. He is seated, hunched, and sunk into himself, like an old man, in a pose of despair and disgust. It is clear that the card shows someone who is chained to his money, or someone who is worried about it, concerned about lack of money. To wish to possess riches or to envy riches is as degrading as to be a miser. Whoever thinks of enriching himself neglects all other gifts and ends up cheapening his soul. This card's meaning is also a valuable pointer to old habits to which we have become enslaved.

Upright: The traditional meaning is a little hard: the card is also sometimes called "the brown youth" or "apprentice." Its meanings include a youth, a workman, a blindman's guide, the enriching of the ignorant, and a profiteer, having to scrape together the means to live. Also, a student, a dark-haired young man, your daily work.

Unfavorable or reversed: Dissipation, ruin, infamy, bad companions, and undesirable habits. Also, criminal profiteering, prodigality (usually with someone else's money), the pursuit of luxury, a placement at a college or an apprenticeship at work.

KNIGHT *of* SHEKELS

The Knight of Shekels is attuned with the second house of the horoscope and also with Taurus, which governs possessions and finances. In Tarot Médiéval, the card shows a black destrier. The horse is still and steady, although the three other knights of the Tarot are in motion. Here the Knight Shekels is on guard, so that no one steals his treasure.

Each of the Tarot's cards has a superior meaning. Here it shows that it is not money itself that brings evil, but rather the love of money, which is the root of all evil. The parable of the Ten Talents shows that man is blameworthy if he does not govern his material life well. The highest spirituality demands that everyone earns his living by honestly facing his responsibilities; it is a mistake to suppose that a religious life dispenses us from legitimate activity. The great mystics like St. Francis of Assisi, St. Catherine of Siena, and St. Theresa of Avila were unremitting workers and organizers of staggering efficiency.

Upright: The traditional meaning of this card follows this same theme: gain, profit, interest. Also, a banker, financier, stockbroker, an obliging person. And for events: duties fulfilled, debts that have been settled, maintaining the means to live, keeping up appearances.

Unfavorable or reversed: Laziness, inactivity, idleness, loss, disillusionment, living parasitically upon the resources of others. Also, a period of unemployment, leisure, inactivity, or inertia. Discouragement or stagnation.

QUEEN *of* SHEKELS

This card, with the King of Shekels, belongs to the sign of Capricorn, and to the tenth house, as well as to the triplicity of earth. The meanings turn upon questions of materiality and or ceremony. The Queen of Shekels, like the King, is sumptuously dressed, with a purple robe that is embroidered with pearls.

The expressions of the four queens show their character: the Queen of Scepters is etherial and spiritual, the Queen of Swords is sad but resolute, the Queen of Cups is gracious and hospitable, the Queen of Shekels is cold and lofty. This arcana represents the value of protecting your place and position in the world. In the Middle Ages, a well-brought-up woman who could not maintain a certain air was condemned by others sharing her status in life. In the same way today, a woman must not fall into vulgarity and crass pleasures. It is her duty to inspire and elevate, not to come down to the level of others. The Queen of Shekels maintains her own dignity and standing, able to provision, support, and use her influence to relieve want.

Upright: In the best sense, this card speaks about the best use of your talents or the gifts that you possess. It also indicates gain, profit, someone who works in a bank, or a financial adviser or investor, someone of confidence, liberality, or opulence. Upkeeping your status and responsibilities. Relieving want and need. Resourcefulness, an honorable life. Also, a significator for a dark-haired woman.

Unfavorable or reversed: Neglected duties, stagnation, laziness, those who seek the help of others, discouragement, and disillusion. Also, indecision, uncertainty, apprehension, and perplexity.

KING *of* SHEKELS

This card dominates the four characters in the Temple of Shekels, ruled by Capricorn, the tenth house of the horoscope, and the earth triplicity. The Temple of Shekels is used only for material questions. The King of Shekels is heavily and richly dressed in a purple robe that is covered with precious jewels. He alone among the four kings demonstrates his riches. The faces of the four kinds indicate their character: the spiritual King of Scepters has a pale, even emaciated, face; the King of Swords has the look of a determined warrior; the King of Cups, the Priest-King and Initiator, has a benign look; the King of Shekels is hard, villainous, and looks like a tyrant. This king must be the master of everything around him, whether above or below. Some imagine that a tyrant is better than the tyranny of the crowd: while others believe no regime is more terrifying than the power of the masses. But it is not possible to steer a boat without a captain, nor a plan without a head. Some hierarchy is essential. The true meaning of the King of Shekels is a businessman—whether an individual, an association, or a state—who is able to buy raw materials, construct factories, risk great losses, so that the workers receive their wages.

Upright: The card represents the investor, the boss, the master, an industrialist, also power, authority, mastery, and is often associated with hardships. Someone who likes and expects value for money. Professional organisations, and national leadership. Also, a significator for a dark-haired man.

Unfavorable or reversed: Injustice, a seedy affair, a defective system, abuse of power and favoritism. According to ancient traditions, someone whose limbs are ailing or who has another kind of physical disability. Tyranny, hard-fisted employers, deals and contracts that tie down your options. Also, someone who profits from others' labors.

PART TWO

WORKING WITH THE TAROT MÉDIÉVAL

By Caitlín Matthews

The Tarot is a field of the mysteries,
and the master of tarot is one who knows how to see
—and enables others to see—the beauty
of its initiatory teaching.

—Francis Rolt-Wheeler:
from "The Temple of Cups" commentary

CHAPTER 3

THE MAGICAL BACKGROUND TO *TAROT MÉDIÉVAL*

The Magical Linage of *TAROT MÉDIÉVAL*

Tarot Mediéval stems from a branch of Tarot that was started by Oswald Wirth, fed by the stream of the French esoteric tradition. Because it has developed slightly differently from more familiar Tarots still used today, it is worth exploring its immediate forebears, as this will help explain where Francis Rolt-Wheeler was coming from.

Oswald Wirth (1860–1943) was a Swiss esotericist who studied symbolism with the French Rosicrucian kabbalist, Stanislas de Guaita (1861–1897). In 1889, Wirth brought out his own 22 card, majors-only, Tarot, Les 22 Arcanes du Tarot Kabbalistique, which consciously incorporated esoteric symbolism into the Tarot de Marseilles—until then, the main Tarot still being continuously produced outside Italy. Wirth's own influences had their roots in the European esoteric tradition that had blossomed over the course of the nineteenth century, drawing upon Freemasonary, especially French Martinist freemasonic imagery, as well as upon the magical and kabbalistic writings of Eliphas Lévi (Alphonse Louis Constant, 1810–1875), and of Papus (Gerald Encausse, 1865–1916), as well as upon the esoteric and initiatory speculations of Paul Christian (pseudonym of Jean-Baptiste Pitois, 1811–1877), whose 1871 book, *L'Histoire de la Magie* or The History of Magic, depicted the Tarot as deriving from a

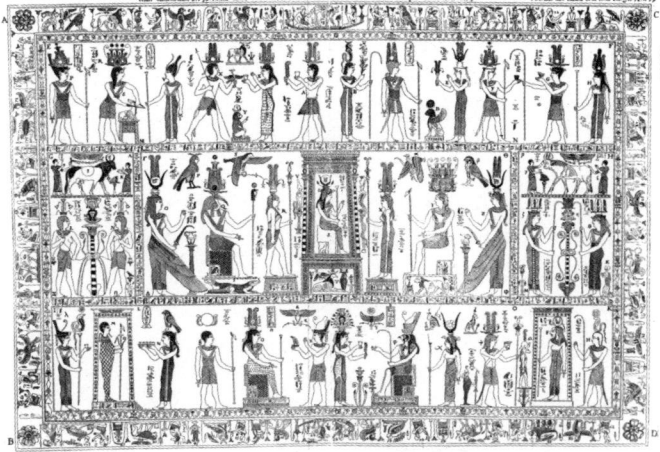

FIG. 1. *An engraving made in 1608 of the Bembine Tablet, a first-century Roman depiction of Egyptian divinities. The tablet itself is now housed in Museo Egizio at Turin, Italy.*

series of initiatory panels within the crypts of the great Pyramid of Memphis.

Alas, no such panels have ever been found, because they were from Christian's own inventive meditations—although he may have had in mind the Bembine Tablet of Isis when he wrote this. The Bembine Tablet is a bronze tablet, dating from the Roman occupation of Egypt. It is also possible that Christian may have read the words of the early nineteenth-century translator Thomas Taylor, the Platonist, who presented a similar scenario of a much-earlier thinker:

"Plato was initiated into the "Greater Mysteries" at the age of 49. The initiation took place in one of the subterranean halls of the Great Pyramid in Egypt. The Isaiac Table (a.k.a., the Bembine Tablet) formed the altar, before which the Divine Plato stood. . . . He was received by the Hierophant of the Pyramid. . . and given verbally the Highest Esoteric Teachings, each accompanied with Its appropriate Symbol."[14]

In 1927, when Wirth later republished his Tarot as Le Tarot des Imagiers du Moyen Age (Tarot of the Medieval Crafts- people), he had clearly overthrown any adherence to the Egyptian origin theory, since it had been conclusively proved by archaeology that these Egyptian speculations about Tarot were spurious; in the second edition of his Tarot and the book that accompanied it, Wirth consciously reached back into the Middle Ages for more plausible originations of the Tarot: to the creators of the medieval cathedrals, and the builders who worked in stone and glass, as well as those craftspeople who worked in tapestry, vellum, and paint, mindful of the living book of symbolism that those cathedrals provided to the faithful. The culture of the Middle Ages was both a safer era in which to couch Wirth's ideas, being truly much nearer to real origins of Tarot. Rolt-Wheeler followed in Wirth's footsteps by espousing a medieval Tarot origin, though he also entertains a wide range of speculative tributaries that descend into the great river of Tarot.

To fully understand how any Egyptian origin was ever imputed to the Tarot, we have to go even further back in time in order to see how the Tarot developed into an esoteric tool for individual readers and magical orders. It may come as a great shock to learn that the very first Tarots, like the fifteenth-century Visconti and Ferrarese Tarots, were not esoteric in nature at all. That development still lay ahead in the eighteenth century. For medieval people, Tarot was still a method of gaming and card-playing, and occasionally of courtly poetry, while some cards were also being used for love spells, curses, and folk magic.[15] We have little or no evidence of divination with Tarot before the eighteenth century, and that's a fact.

The game of Tarot spread out of Italy to most places in Europe, but especially into France where, in the late seventeenth and early eighteenth centuries, French printers produced a style of Tarot we now know as the Tarot de Marseilles. In 1781, the Swiss antiquarian Antoine Court de Gebelin was exploring the roots of sacred traditions. He wrote in his *Le Monde Primitif*: "There exists today a work of the ancient Egyptians, one of the books saved from the flames which destroyed their superb libraries... The sole survivor... it is so well known that there is no learned man who has not deigned to look into it, no-one before guessing at its pictorial origin. That book is the Game of Tarot."[16] The idea of a pack of cards as a set of flash cards of a once profound spiritual tradition—a book of wisdom in card form—became a very popular and inspiring notion, with many people attempting to crack that "ancient code of wisdom." According to Lévi, the prisoner in solitary confinement armed with simply a deck of Tarot cards would have "access to all knowledge."[17] This was an enchanting notion.

Following Court de Gebelin came the man we can seriously call the "Father of Cartomancy": Etteilla, or Jean Baptiste Alliette (1738–1791), who brought out a series of card decks, including a Tarot that consciously drew upon de Gebelin's esoteric symbolism, and that taught people cartomancy, or the art of divining by cards. This art quickly spread across Europe within the course of a mere fifteen to twenty years, aided by the upheavals of the French Revolution, and the movements caused by the Napoleonic wars.

Later, in 1855, into this heady mix of Egyptian origins and esoteric lore, came the self-aggrandizing Eliphas Lévi (1810–1875). Lévi started out as a Catholic ordinand for the priesthood, and briefly entered a Benedictine monastery, before moving sideways from religion into magic, and becoming a ceremonial magician instead. (Rather like Rolt-Wheeler himself, who left his priestly vocation behind in the United States to follow a magical career in France.) It was Lévi who was responsible for realigning the Tarot with the work of the Hermetic magician, diverting it from the route of being a cartomantic divinatory tool, as first popularized by Etteilla. In his book The Doctrine and Rituals of High Magic, Lévi associated together, for the first time, the 22 cards of the major arcana (itself an esoteric title invented by Paul Christian) with the 22 letters of the Hebrew alphabet and, by association, with the 22 paths of the kabbalistic Tree of Life. Levi also associated the four suits of Tarot with the Tetragrammaton, or the Holy Name of God, and with the four emanatory worlds of Kabbalah. This is why so many Tarots today refer to Kabbalah so frequently, despite the fact that Lévi made many grandiose and unsubstantiated claims for his rather shaky Hebraic research. Needless to say, none of these theories had previously been associated with Tarot. Lévi himself drew upon the somewhat partial kabbalistic research of the seventeenth-century German Jesuit and polymath Athansius Kircher (1616–1680).

All these ideas fueled the creation of many magical orders anxious to further explore this esoteric tradition across Europe, where eclectic magical groups sprang up, some claiming highfalutin origins and hierarchic titles for themselves, while others more modestly meditated their way to knowledge. In 1888, in Britain, the mother and father of all esoteric orders and fellowships, the Hermetic Order of the Golden Dawn, was born, blazed brightly, and fizzled out in a scandal of acrimony and counteraccusation. This order worked with magical principles, kabbalistic lore, and the Tarot in a far more systematic way, creating an initiatory pathway that is still largely followed by its many offshoots, now distributed all over the world.

Meanwhile, in the United States a parallel tradition was unfolding that led to the creation of yet another Oswald Wirth–style deck. John Augustus Knapp (1853–1938) was an artist and a mason who collaborated with Manly P. Hall on the creation of a compendious book about the esoteric background for the Western Mystery tradition: The Secret Teachings of All Ages (1928). Manley P. Hall (1901–1990) himself was the founder of the Philosophical Research Society, which was established in 1934 in Los Angeles. In 1929, Hall and Knapp together brought out The Revised New Art Tarot, which followed the Wirth-style Tarot values, but added a minor arcana of 56 cards to the 22 major trumps, making it the first full Wirth-style Tarot. The minor cards in this pack are arranged in various geometric ways, with meditation symbols on each of the number cards—a feature that we also see in the design of Tarot Médiéval. Furthermore, on each of the trumps and court cards is a further symbol in a shield, also for meditation. These cards were reissued again recently in 2013 and are still used by several magical groups as a method of magical training.

There was also a further Wirth-style deck that we must not neglect: the Lasenic Tarot, made in Czechoslovakia in 1938, designed by Pierre de Lasenic (Petr Pavel Kohout, 1900–1944), and illustrated by Vladislav Kužel. Lasenic was a student of Oswald Wirth and a member of many esoteric groups. Lasenic's writings gave him a difficult reputation at a time when esoteric work was regarded as a suspect, if not a criminal activity. His membership of Universalia, a popular esoteric association, later brought him into conflict after the German occupation, since all esoteric group meetings were banned by the Nazi administration, as was his monthly magazine, Medium. As with Rolt-Wheeler's Tarot Médiéval, the publication date of the Lasenic Tarot was situated in the most difficult of years, as Czechoslovakia became annexed by the Nazis in 1938, triggering the beginning of World War II. Like his confrères in Britain who took their spiritual resources to war, Lasenic and other members of Universalia used meditation and ritual to astrally work against Hitler in a practical example of a well-organized magical operation.[18] So, what distinguishes an Oswald Wirth–style Tarot from other Tarots? You can be certain that you are using such a Tarot if all or some of the following appear on your cards:

- The Fool has a lynx pursuing him and a crocodile in front of him.

- On the Magician's table is a large coin, which he is touching, and a sword and chalice. In his hand is a double-ended wand with red and blue tips.

- The Priestess holds two keys and has a crescent moon on her crown's top.

- The Hermit holds a seven-sectioned, bamboo-like staff, while a serpent moves before him on the path.

- A butterfly upon a red rose in the Star, or a white lily in the Empress card.

- A red tulip in different stages of growth can be found in the cards of the Emperor, Temperance, Magician, and Fool.

Today, in an era when we have a more Tarots than we know which to choose, it is worth remembering that the first half of the twentieth century was not so blessed for choice. There was the Oswald Wirth deck in 1889, which was reissued in 1929, and the Rider Waite-Smith Tarot of 1909; then the Knap-Hall deck of 1929; and then the Larsenic Tarot, published in 1938 by Pierre de Lasenic and drawn by Vladislav Kuzel (1898–1965), and a handful of others, but unless you were travelling in Italy, where regional

Tarots were available, your choice range was limited.

In bringing to publication the Tarot Médiéval, Francis Rolt-Wheeler and Christian Loring were consciously creating a new and more romantic imagery to Tarot, synthesizing the esoteric ideas of the late nineteenth and early twentieth century, but couching them within the late medieval styles of Italian Tarot that were the very first to grace the world. In creating the text for the Tarot, Rolt-Wheeler largely drew upon his own correspondence course on the Tarot, Kabbalah, and the way of initiation, *Le Cabbalisme Initiatique* (3 volumes), which was published between 1936 and 1940. He also drew heavily upon a pair of popular books written when Rolt-Wheeler was still living in the United States—*The Key to the Universe* and *The Key to Destiny*, written by Harriette Augusta Curtiss and F. Homer Curtiss in 1917. These books revealed and described the Tarot in one of the first public amplifications of Tarot as an initiatic path, and many points are copied over into Tarot Médiéval from these books, notably the symbols and titles of the major arcana, and the numerology of each card.

Was Rolt-Wheeler himself a magician, we may ask? Like many of those mentioned above in this short history, he was a man interested in following the esoteric path and keen to inform, instruct, and encourage others to do so. His esoteric magazine *Astrosophie* kept going from 1929 to 1958, apart from the war years when such things were banned by the Nazis. Written largely by himself, but with articles syndicated or translated from other esoteric magazines, *l'Astrosophie* was full of his own articles on everything from prayer to meditation, and from astrological predictions about upcoming events before World War II, to the intentions of salient political figures of the time. From this we can see that Rolt-Wheeler was no armchair occultist, but fully immersed in high esoteric principles. He ran several correspondence courses upon the main training topics of esotericism: Tarot, Kabbalah, astrology. He kept in touch with esoteric trends, writers, and cultural figures all over the Western world. It is clear to the reader that Rolt-Wheeler himself was not fully conversant with Tarot history since, at one point, he spoke of "pre-Christian" versions of the Priestess/Papesse card: of course, there are no versions of any Tarot before the early fifteenth century, as this is when they first arise in Italy—showing how pervasive was the idea of the Bembine Tablet and Egyptian origins in French esoteric thought!

Rolt-Wheeler was more of an inspirer and torchbearer for esoteric work, a latter-day librarian of lost texts, a keeper and custodian of the teachings that the library of Alexandria—destroyed in the first century CE—would have both housed and honored. His own formal magical training may have derived from a mixture of masonic or magical instruction, but we cannot fully attest to which groups he belonged. Rolt-Wheeler largely followed his own path, making an eclectic mélange of magical lore, medieval Christian, and pagan imagery in his descriptions of the cards, as well as drawing upon the mainstream Oswald Wirth/French school of esoteric thought for his chief inspiration.

The medieval vision upon which Christian Loring drew for her art was clearly one with which he was highly sympathetic, perhaps inspired by Wirth's reissue of his Tarot based upon the "craftspeople of the middle ages." His harsh words about the garish and grotesque renditions of Tarot art (c.f. p. 14) stem from the poor reproductions of Tarots available in his era, and from the sometimes crudely worked woodcuts of earlier times. He was clearly not inspired by the innovations of Pamela Coleman Smith's art style, which, despite being illustrated with figures dressed in medieval costume, was painted in a very modern style. Rolt-Wheeler speaks with a deep yearning for the Middle Ages, despite the welter of nineteenth-century-inspired esoteric lore that he wraps around his Tarot. Living in France, he could not but be deeply aware of the medieval heritage of his adoptive country, and how widely it had influenced European history and culture. It is, of course, an idealized vision, based more upon the mythic tales of the Matière de France, of Charlemagne and Roland, and on the stories of his own birth right, the Matière de Britain, of King Arthur and the Grail legends. How he must have clung to these myths in the wake of the coming war, when Europe's civilizing cultural light was darkening and diminishing, as Fascism spread its widening ripples of brutality—gripping everyone with alarm and uncertainty, and how he must have upheld the torch of the magical tradition with both hands, to stave off the darkness that threatened the world.

WHY THE KABBALAH?

Over the last two hundred years, the Tarot has accumulated quantities of esoteric lore and symbolic attributions, to the point where any sensible Tarot reader is likely to become alienated or confused: indeed, the margins of some very esoteric Tarot cards often pullulate with competing symbols, to the point when the main image on the card itself seems to retreat into insignificance. Of all the astrological, mythic, and other lore the Tarot has attracted, none has been more contentious than the ascription of kabbalistic symbolism to the Tarot. The Tarot's date of origination lies around 1425 in northern Italy, so what is Kabbalah, and what on earth does it have to do with the Tarot? I will attempt to succinctly disentangle the two, so that the reader will have the apparatus to understand why it appears in *Tarot Médiéval*.

Kabbalah is the study of the mystical lore of the universe, which lies at the heart of Jewish mystical thought. The abstractions, symbols, and concepts of this thought and its connections are all tabulated upon the template of a tree, the Otz Chaim or the Tree of Life. This plan of the Tree of Life provides a meditational map to students of Kabbalah, whereby its diagrammatic two-dimensionality on paper is intended to become three-dimensional (or more) within the human imagination. By study of these principles, and their connections, the kabbalist creates a closer union between him- or herself and the divine, so that he or she might live on earth with virtue and a sense of service. Besides its devotional side, Jewish Kabbalah also has its own mystical practice, which differs from the study of Hermetic Qabala (see below).

The flow of power upon the Tree of Life emanates from the Divine, perceived as lying behind the Ain (unmanifest or nothingness), the Ain Soph (limitlessness), and the Ain Soph Aur (infinite light): this power is mediated down to the earthly plane, held by and passing through ten reservoirs or vessels called sephiroth, as Rolt-Wheeler tells us:

"Here is a brief description of the Sephiroth to give a key to the reader: first of all stands the *Ain* or Absolute, which, becoming conscious, in turn reveals the *Ain Soph* or Divine Wisdom, which exteriorizes in the *Ain Soph Aur* or the Infinite Light. From this triune source stem the ten sephiroth:

1. Kether—the supreme crown

2. Chockmah—perfect wisdom

3. Binah—perfect understanding

4. Chesed—perfect power

5. Geburah—perfect justice

6. Tiphareth—perfect beauty

7. Netzach—perfect love

8. Hod—perfect intelligence

9. Yesod—the Formation, the astral sphere

10. Malkuth—the Foundation, the material sphere"

Each sephira—the singular name of the plural "sephiroth"—contains one of the emanations of the divine power. Connecting each of the sephiroth are a series of 22 pathways leading between them, which have always been used as meditational aids to comprehending the qualities of each sephira: by elevating the soul, the kabbalist seeks to not only understand but to mediate these qualities in his life and on behalf of his community.

As to how the Tarot became associated with the Kabbalah, we have to understand the route by which Kabbalah came to be part of Western esoteric thought. There are many different schools of Jewish Kabbalah that continue to this day, but here we are concerned with Hermetic or Christian Qabala (I use this spelling to distinguish Jewish from gentile usage), which arose a lot later, with the help of the fifteenth-century Italian humanist scholar Pico della Mirandola (1463–1494); he attempted to reconcile kabbalism and Neo-Platonism with Christianity, and his influential writings on Hermeticism and Kabbalah created a flood of interest at a time when the beliefs of the Christian West were fast approaching Reformation, so that many scholars became familiar with its tenets.

A century further on, the German Jesuit and polymath Athanasius Kircher received kabbalistic ideas with the same enthusiasm as he took interest in Egyptian hieroglyphics, Hermetic ideas, and the Greek philosophy with which he larded his work. Kircher's studies were an attempt to arrive at an ecumenical viewpoint of world religions in history by making comparisons between these and Christianity. However, his own understanding of Kabbalah, depicted in his Oedipus Aegyptiacus, spurned authentic Jewish kabbalistic understandings; his version of the Tree of Life appeared with associated letters of the Hebrew alphabet ascribed to each of the sephiroth, but alongside the celestial orders, the classical planets, and so on. His individual and eclectic understandings were to lay down a foundation for Hermetic Qabala, which is still at some variance from Jewish kabbalistic study, but it would go further and become more complex yet. While Kircher's planetary ascriptions to the Tree of Life were to become a standard part of Western esoteric thought, his Hebraic ascriptions to the Tree were to suffer yet further permutations over the centuries. From such studies of Hermeticism there arose from the wreck of the Reformation the Rosicrucian movement of 1614, where the attractive idea of the hidden wisdom of the ages was merged together with the notion of groups of hidden initiates, further fueling the creation of Freemasonry: here the Mysteries were reborn within the Western world, and from the fusion of all these ideas, we receive modern Hermetic magic.[19]

What now seem standard esoteric associations of the Tarot with the Kabbalah arose only in the eighteenth century with the coming of the French esoteric revival. Antoine Court de Gebelin was a Swiss savant and freemason who posited in his nine-volume Le Monde Primitif, a golden age in antiquity in which primitive humanity shared a common language, culture, and religion, from which every subsequent civilization descended. This idea has subsequently proved very popular, both in sensationist speculations on the ancient world, as well as upon the more temperate study of the Perennial Tradition. In volume VIII of this work, de Gebelin reports how he intuitively understood the Tarot as "an Egyptian Book escaped from barbarism" and from the accidents of time.[20] He also erroneously declared that the 22 trumps were numerated by letters that were common to the Egyptian and Hebrew alphabets. However, while Hebrew may have 22 letters, the Egyptian alphabet does not. Such is the vagary of fate, that Court de Gébelin's rambling discourse was taken up by a French fellow mason, the Comte de Mellet (1727–1804), whose own essay on the Tarot further associated the Hebrew alphabet with the Tarot trumps, but in a very different order.

Following ideas outlined in the work of Athanasius Kircher,

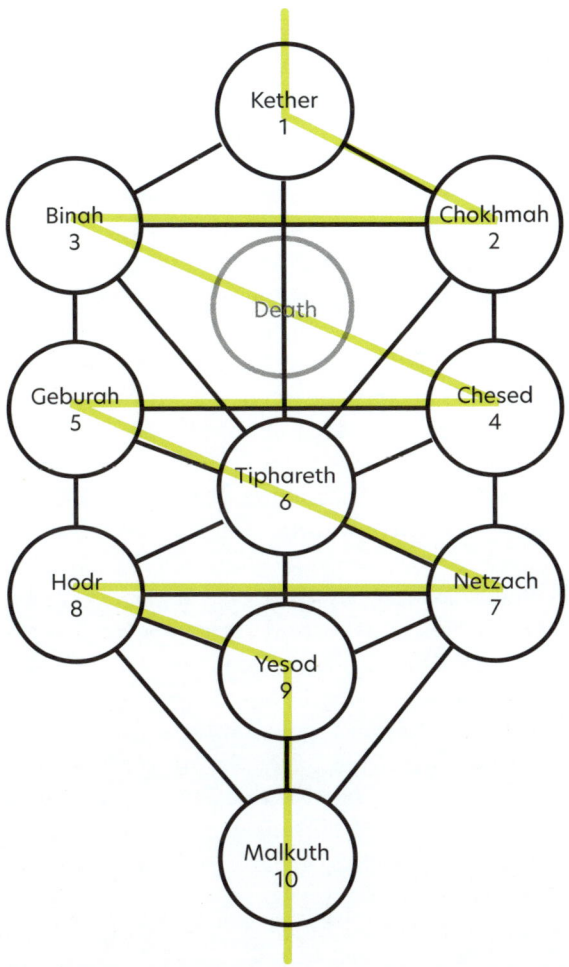

FIG. 2. The Otz Chaim or Tree of Life, here shown with the lightning flash—the divine flow of power down the tree—and the mysterious sephira of Da'ath or Knowledge that is hidden. https://commons.wikimedia.org/wiki/Category:Tree_of_life_(Kabbalah)#/media/File:Tree_of_life_wk_02.svg

it was the magician Éliphas Lévi who ascribed the 22 Tarot trumps to the paths connecting the sephiroth or spheres of the Tree of Life, working up a magical system in which both Kabbalah and Tarot featured. Later on, the British magician Samuel McGregor Mathers (1854–1918) of the Hermetic Order of the Golden Dawn changed Lévi's method of kabbalistic association on the Tarot, while the Oswald Wirth school of Tarots still followed the Éliphas Lévi method. The Golden Dawn also wrought further changes to Lévi's system by assigning the number zero to the Fool, rather than placing it between Judgement and the World as Lévi had done: this caused all the Tarot ascriptions to the Hebrew alphabet to move down by one letter, with the result that you can see in fig. 3. Furthermore, the Golden Dawn swapped round the cards VIII Justice with XI Strength, so that Strength with its lion would accord with the astrological ascription of Leo, while Justice and its balances were realigned with Libra. The Rider-Waite-Smith Tarot followed this Golden Dawn trend, and as a result, most modern Tarots now have Justice at position XI and Strength at VIII. Which Hebrew letters were ascribed to each path has varied considerably over the last century and half, but Rolt-Wheeler followed the Lévi and Oswald Wirth ascriptions.

A study of the Qabala is now considered standard in most mystery schools and magical lodges, who will often use a mixture of qabalistic lore, with other mystical knowledge, including that of the Tarot, to train their students. It is something that would have delighted Pico della Mirandola, and probably horrified Athanasius Kircher.

To summarize our brief look at Kabbalah, it is clear from even a very brief study of Jewish Kabbalah that for Orthodox Jewish kabbalists, any graven images such as appear on the Tarot would be abhorrent and utterly contrary to the laws of Moses, which is probably why Éliphas Lévi found it easier to square the association of the Tarot with Egyptian belief, even though it had no such connection, while he still enthusiastically upheld a Jewish background of magic, as he interpreted it.

The Tarot scholar Ronald Dekker has suggested that the retrofitting of Tarot to the Kabbalah might be traced back to Sha'are Ora or the "Gates of Life" by the Castillian kabbalist Joseph Gikatilla (1248–1325), where the author speaks of wells, and treasures, swords and branches, but a closer reading of that influential and devotional text reveals that Gikatilla is referring to the qualities of the sephiroth as symbols of blessings, affliction, and duty, not to the Tarot at all.[21]

As a result of these developments, many modern Tarots have taken on kabbalistic, astrological, numerological, and other correspondences that all threaten to diminish the ability of Tarot cards to speak for themselves, which is probably why so many Tarots have chosen to leave behind traditional pip cards in favor of pictorial images that explicitly convey the meaning of each card by an illustration that the eye can understand, without the need of the mind to struggle to remember so many associated correspondences. Few modern Tarot users are equipped today with the in-depth kabbalistic knowledge to steer through this often-troubled codification of Tarot. Today, most users are more interested in being able to divine from the cards clearly in the way that Etteilla would have been pleased to acknowledge, while there remain a few readers who still harbor a lingering suspicion that the Tarot stems from an Egyptian source, however many times evidence to the contrary is demonstrated.

Card order in Tarot Médiéval:	Hebrew Letters in Tarot Médiéval & Wirth-Style Tarots		Hebrew Letters in Golden-style Tarot	
I Magician	א	ALEPH	ב	BETH
II High Priestess	ב	BETH	ג	GIMEL
III Empress	ג	GIMEL	ד	DALET
IV Emperor	ד	DALET	ה	HEH
V Hierophant	ה	HEH	ו	VAU
VI Lovers	ו	VAU	ז	ZAYIN
VII Chariot	ז	ZAYIN	ח	CHET
VIII Justice	ח	CHET	ל	LAMED
IX Hermit	ט	TETH	י	YOD
X Wheel of Fortune	י	YOD	כ	KAPH
XI Strength	כ	KAPH	ט	TETH
XII Hanged Man	ל	LAMED	מ	MEM
XIII Death	מ	MEM	נ	NUN
XIV Temperance	נ	NUN	ס	SAMECH
XV Devil	ס	SAMECH	ע	AYIN
XVI Tower	ע	AYIN	פ	PEH
XVII Star	פ	PEH	צ	TZADDI
XVIII Moon	צ	TZADDI	ק	QOPH
XIX Sun	ק	QOPH	ר	RESH
XX Judgement	ר	RESH	ש	SHIN
XXI Fool	ש	SHIN	א	ALEPH
XXII World	ת	TAU	ת	TAU

FIG. 3. *A comparison of the ascription of Hebrew letters on Wirth-style Tarots, based on Lévi, and the Golden Dawn–style Tarots*

Card	Hebrew Letters		Path on Tree of Life	Between Sephiorth:
Magician	א	ALEPH	11	1. Kether - 2.Chokmah
High Priestess	ב	BETH	12	1. Kether - 3. Binah
Empress	ג	GIMEL	13	1. Kether - 6.Tiphareth
Emperor	ד	DALET	14	2. Chokmah - 3. Binah
Hierophant	ה	HEH	15	2. Chokmah - 6.Tiphareth
Lovers	ו	VAU	16	2. Chokmah - 4.Chesed
Chariot	ז	ZAYIN	17	3. Binah - 6. Tiphareth
Justice	ח	CHET	18	3. Binah - 5. Geburah
Hermit	ט	TETH	19	4. Chesed - 5.Geburah
Wheel of Fortune	י	YOD	20	4. Chesed - 6.Tiphareth
Strength	כ	KAPH	21	4. Chesed - 7. Netzach
Hanged Man	ל	LAMED	22	5. Geburah - 6. Tiphareth
Death	מ	MEM	23	5. Geburah - 8. Hod
Temperance	נ	NUN	24	6.Tiphareth - 7. Netzach
Devil	ס	SAMECH	25	6.Tiphareth - 9. Yesod
Tower	ע	AYIN	26	6. Tiphareth - 8.Hod
Star	פ	PEH	27	7. Netzach - 8.Hod
Moon	צ	TZADDI	28	7. Netzach - 9. Yesod
Sun	ק	QOPH	29	7. Netzach - 10 Malkuth
Judgement	ר	RESH	30	8. Hod - 9.Yesod
Fool	ש	SHIN	31	8. Hod - 10. Malkuth
World	ת	TAU	32	9. Yesod - 10. Malkuth

FIG. 4. *Major Arcana of Wirth-style Tarots on Tree of Life paths*

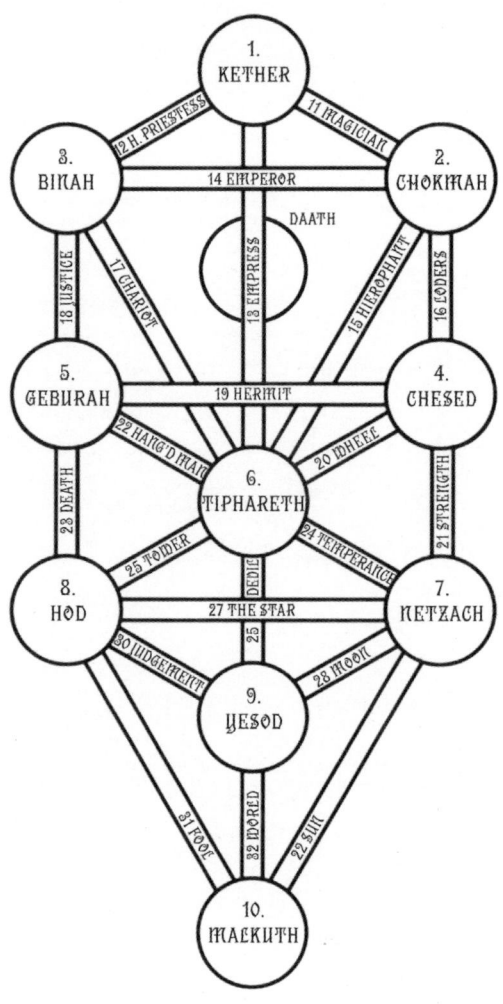

FIG. 5. *Major Arcana of Tarot Médiéval upon the paths*

Working magically with the Tree of Life requires a much deeper study than is given here, of course. So many hands have contributed to this study, often with the desire to associate every last esoteric concept and make it work upon the Tree. In this respect, Rolt-Wheeler was no different from his teachers and colleagues. In his description of the King of Swords, he associates the esoteric planes of Theosophical and Hermetic understanding together in an eclectic way, finding them to

"have a strong relationship to the central pillar on the Tree of Life, where we find four sephiroth: Malkuth, the material sphere of earth; Yesod, the lunar sphere of water, and of the astral and the emotions; Tiphareth, the solar sphere, of the spiritual and redemptive powers, the sphere of fire; and Kether, the etheric sphere of the first stirrings, the sphere of air. There are four planes, just as there are also four worlds: Assiah, Yetzirah, Briah, and Atziluth, which correspond to the planes of earth, water, fire, and air, and with the temples of tarot, with Shekels, Cups, Swords, and Scepters."

Rolt-Wheeler in this book is largely using the Four Worlds and the suits as placeholders for the material, astral, mental, and spiritual planes.

The four worlds of Kabbalah are, of course, much more subtle than such a cursory treatment as this can convey, and while the elemental ascriptions of the suits have been associated with them, I would recommend seeking out a good study of the Kabbalah where they are dealt in more depth. If you wish to follow the Wirth-style Tarot school of thought on this, then read *The Revised New Art-Tarot: Mysticism and Qabalah in the Knapp Hall Tarot* by Yolanda M. Robinson.

THE TAROT AND THE MYSTERIES

Rolt-Wheeler conceived of Tarot Médiéval primarily as an initiatory pathway rather than as a divinatory tool. He tells us that "the tarot, taken as a whole, is a complete teaching on one of the Seven Veils of Initiation. It is in this sense that we are going to direct our interpretation."[22] Throughout his study of the Tarot Médiéval, he continually stresses that "the major arcana should not be used for divination, but rather to establish a principle or tendency, or only in the case of a spiritual question." It may seem baffling to the reader that the Tarot should be treated with such reserve, but then the writer is viewing the Tarot primarily as an initiatory pathway, one that echoes and resonates with the path of the Mysteries. It was believed by many that the power of the major arcana might displace readings on mundane matters, for which the minor arcana was used (see p. 180).

Every spiritual tradition has its own mysteries: these are the central tenets of mystical understanding, whether we look at Christianity with its seven sacraments, or the Mystery religions of the Classical ancient world.

The Mystery cults of the Classical ancient world, like those at Eleusis, in Asia Minor, or Alexandria, were a ritualized response to the spiritual pathways that the gods opened for humanity. At Eleusis, near Athens, the mysteries of Demeter the mother and her daughter, Persephone, were acted out on a seasonal basis: the initiation offered in the autumn was called the Lesser Mysteries and was given to candidates who aligned themselves with the myth of Persephone's descent into the underworld at the time when the crops were harvested. This enabled the candidate to understand the requirement for the earth to be made fertile and ready for cultivation, at a basic level, but at a more mystical level, through a ritual embodiment of Persephone's descent and her mother's urgent search. They also understood the principle of the soul's descent into the darkness of death and withdrawal in order to be reborn.

In the Spring rites, when the Greater Mysteries were celebrated, those who had been initiated into the autumn's Lesser Mysteries might more deeply understand what is required on the spiritual path. These more profound mysteries were never explicated or written down, for silence was the promise that each of its initiates kept, but these rites brought each soul into deeper communion with divine understanding. It is from Demeter that humanity learns the art of agricultural cultivation, but it is from the descent of Persephone that the rebirth of the soul becomes a living myth to inspire. Very much like the digging of a garden to prepare for planting the seeds, and the final flowering of a plant, these ancient mysteries required preparatory purification, an alignment with the heart of the myth before the revelation of the mystery might be received.

We may gain some insight into the nature of these mysteries from the initiations taken within Christianity, wherein a child is first baptized into the Christian family, becoming the kindred of Christ; yet at confirmation, that same child—now older and prepared by instruction—can partake of the Eucharist and understand what it is to have "Christ within." These initiations are different from those undertaken in either Classical mystery schools or modern initiations into magical orders, but we can nonetheless perceive the pattern of the mysteries as one of a serial and deepening induction into the life of the church, where people become united with each other in the sacrament of matrimony, or where the devoted become ordained as priests or are clothed as religious in monastic orders. These are all initiations.

The Classical model of the Lesser and Greater Mysteries became the pattern for initiation within magical lodges and circles, whereby an applicant (the neophyte) was brought into the lodge and instructed in the secret teachings of the esoteric arts through a series of initiations. It is in this way that Rolt-Wheeler understands the Tarot. For him, the cards of the minor arcana represent the Lesser Mysteries whereby we tread the fourfold path of the elements: the four suits of Swords, Scepters, Cups, and Shekels or Coins. For him, the major arcana represents the Greater Mysteries, which leads us more deeply into communion with the archetypes and myths of esoteric understanding.

In actuality, the terms "major and minor arcana" were first used in 1871 by the French esotericist Paul Christian, in his book *Histoire de Magie*, where he took up the idea of the Tarot as a tool of magical enlightenment. Following him, in Britain, the Hermetic Order of the Golden Dawn instructed its neophytes to create their own Tarot cards in order to better understand the Tree of Life and their place upon it. As we have seen, the 22 paths of the Tree of Life and its 10 sephiroth also represent an initiatory way of progress: meditation upon the sephiroth and path-walking the 22 paths of the Tree were practical methods of understanding the cosmic patterns as patterned within Tarot.

Lodges and magical groups have many different kinds of initiation ceremonies, which act as markers upon the royal road of service. Most of these initiatory forms have been inherited from the Classical and Gnostic mysteries, whereby the neophyte ascends through different grades that are based upon the planetary vices and virtues: within Gnostic and Mithraic ceremonies, the candidate ascended the klimax heptapulos or seven-fold ladder of the Classical planets, arriving at the eighth position in a more mature and well-tested state of being. This path parallels the many schools that draw upon the kabbalistic model of the Tree of Life, which also has seven levels.

The parade of the major arcana, like a great medieval procession, unfolds matters of more serious weight than the minor arcana with their pip and court cards speaking of more everyday matters, but that doesn't mean to say that we cannot ask questions of both the arcana.

In his commentary upon the Hierophant, Rolt-Wheeler reveals to us the three essential things that are required to be an initiate:

1. A theoretical knowledge of the divine plan, the processes of spiritual evolution, and the practical power to bring harmony to this evolution.

2. A theoretical knowledge of the role that must be played by humanity in this evolution, including the duty required of a generation, a country, a group of people and of neophytes themselves, with the practical power to accomplish their own part by helping their fraternity.

3. A profound knowledge of esoteric and mystical principles, with the acquired power to travel upon the spiritual planes where one can be put in touch with the Higher Powers, before consciously receiving the teaching that will be finally transmitted to other human beings. It is clear that the stream cannot climb higher than its source, and that humanity cannot be lifted up if the evolutionary power is not constantly nourished from on high.

He speaks of the sevenfold guardians of initiations:

"There are seven gears which direct the dynamic energy of the Universe, and the man who can handle these seven gears must overtake the state of struggle to gain a calm self-control. It is not only the overcoming of matter, but the control of matter itself. It is necessary to acquire a triple self-control of oneself: body, soul, and spirit, on the four worlds which are within each of us. It is a spiritual victory over the material plane. It is worth noting that the teachings of tarot do not permit ascetic practices in order to bring victory over the physical body; it is not permitted to restrict teachings which would diminish the mental powers; it is especially not permitted to forget spiritual work, which enables the health of the spirit."

Upon the initiatory path, there are many pitfalls. Rolt-Wheeler exemplifies this for us by taking the Moon card and commenting upon its twin canines of Dog and Wolf—echoing the French expression for twilight, "entre chien et loup" or "between dog and wolf," indicating the unchancy inability to tell between the two of them easily by shape or color in the half-light—and the pitfall that the crayfish in the water holds for us:

The neophyte has to conquer the three flatteries of the dog:

1. The false and sycophantic friends who seek to gain something from him for themselves.
2. A excessive sense of self-satisfaction.
3. The temptation to succeed by which the dark forces seek to bring him down.

Then the neophyte must conquer the three hostilities of the wolf:

1. The obvious enemy who does both to hide his enmity.
2. Cruelty within oneself.
3. The active hatred of the brotherhood of shadows who seek to intimidate him.

Then the neophyte must overcome the three temptations of the crayfish:

1. The habitual values of her family, class, or race.
2. The apparently trivial habits of life, which are like iron manacles.

3. The primitive sensuality that lurks always near the surface and against which she must be vigilant in moments of inattention.

In such a way, the author provides clear guidance as to how we might work with each card in an initiatory way.

Borrowing a schema directly from Paul Christian's 1871 *Histoire de la Magie* or History of Magic, Rolt-Wheeler sees the first nine arcana as touching upon the interior life of the neophyte; while the nine following arcana reveal the active life of the Initiate. The last quartet of the major arcana is made up of XIX Sun, XX Judgement, XXI The World, and XXII The Fool. Of the two groups of nine cards, the first group lead us into personal initiation (I–IX) and the second group (X–XVIII) reveal the evolution of the aspiration in his rapport with others; they are followed by the quartet of cards that concern the spiritual alchemy that is known by the name the Great Alchemical Work. As the reader will note, the numbers of each of the cards in the Lesser Mysteries line are also the sum of the numbers in the Greater Mysteries line: e.g., Temperance is 14 and $1 + 4 = 5$ the number of Hierophant or pope, or Justice 8 is echoed in Star's 17, $1 + 7 = 8$. Thus, this card creates pairs of related initiations and steps upon the path.

THE INNER LIFE OF THE NEOPHYTE: THE LESSER MYSTERIES	THE ACTIVE LIFE OF THE INITIATE: THE GREATER MYSTERIES	THE GREAT ALCHEMICAL WORK:
1 Magician	10 Wheel of Fortune	19 Sun
2 High Priestess	11 Strength	20 Judgement
3 Empress	12 Hanged Man	21 Fool
4 Emperor	13 Death	22 World
5 Pope	14 Temperance	
6 Lovers	15 Devil	
7 Chariot	16 Tower	
8 Justice	17 Star	
9 Hermit	18 Moon	

FIG. 6. *The initiatory patterns of the Major Arcana*

As we can see from the following chart, we each learn to govern ourselves on the path of the Lesser Mysteries so that so we may know how to balance the corresponding forces in the Greater Mysteries. The Great Work is completed when the horizonal path of the Lesser Mysteries has enabled the vertical path of the Greater Mysteries: upon the cross that this makes, the Rose of the Mysteries can bloom at last.

LESSER MYSTERIES	INITIATORY TASKS
I Magician	Learning the tools of the craft; receiving from above, bestowing upon all below
II Priestess	Learning the secrets of the mystery; synthesising written and oral knowledge discreetly and honoring the truth
III Empress	Learning mental evocation by creative imagination; understanding the spiritual evolution of matter.
IV Emperor	Learning how to manifest and transform spiritual forces
V Hierophant	Coordinating the balance of spiritual force, the power of action, knowledge, and opportunity, with service
VI Lovers	Learning about free will; discovering responsibility for one's choices and actions, about the working of polarity in ritual.
VII Chariot	Learning how to balance the path of life with serenity.
VIII Justice	Learning how to bring order to chaos by just action.
IX Hermit	Learning from silence, sharing the light to guide others.

GREATER MYSTERIES	INITIATORY TASKS
X Wheel	Learning to turn the wheel of magic, to vitalize life in action
XI Strength	Learning to uphold morality: becoming part of the golden chain of initiates.
XII Hanged Man	Learning to spend our spiritual treasure: dedication to the work.
XIII Death	Learning to transform matter into spirit.
XIV Temperance	Learning self-mastery; how to temper past lives with the present one.

FIG. 7. *The initiations of the Major Arcana*

XV Devil	Learning how to avoid the temptations of self-indulgence and spiritual self-sabotage.
XVI Tower	Learning to overcome pride and presumption.
XVII Star	Learning to reveal the soul's beauty; nourishing the soul with hope.
XVIII Moon	Learning to decern illusions; conquering ambition, flattery and hostility.

THE GREAT WORK	INITIATORY TASKS
XIX Sun	Transmuting the soul to gold; joy, spiritual strength and love.
XX Judgement	Transmuting death into eternal life; liberation, healing, rebirth.
XXI Fool	Transmuting ignorance into intelligence, agitation into tranquillity.
XXII World	Transmuting the spiritual into the divine: completing the path.

FIG. 7. *The initiations of the Major Arcana (cont'd)*

MEDITATION WITH THE CARDS

The Initiatory powers of the major arcana are also figured in Rolt-Wheeler's titles: for example, XVII The Star is called "the Daughter of the Firmament" or "That Which Lives between the Waters." While each card's title comes largely from the Oswald Wirth's Tarot of the Bohemians, the magical titles of each major arcana derive from MacGregor Mather's Book T, and the Golden Dawn system of Tarot, showing that Rolt-Wheeler was quite capable of mixing the French and English magical systems.

Card	Rolt-Wheeler Titles:	McGregor-Mathers' Titles:
I Magician	Powerful Magician	Magus of Power
II Priestess	Priestess of the Stars	Priestess of the Silver Star
III Empress	Daughter of the Almighty	Daughter of the Mighty Ones, Sun/Son of the Morning
IV Emperor	Chief of the Powerful	Chief Among the Mighty
V Hierophant	Mage of Eternity	Magus of the Eternal, Children of the Voice
VI Lovers	Oracle of Two Powerfil Gods	Oracle of the Mighty Children of the Voice
VII Chariot	Lord of Triumph and Light	Lord of the Triumph of Light
VIII Justice	Daughter of the Lords of Truth	Ruler of the Balance
IX Hermit	Prophet of Eternity, of the Word of Power	Magus of the Voice of Power
X Wheel of Fortune	Lord of the Powers of Life	Lord of the Forces of Life, Daughter of the Lords of Truth
XI Strength	Daughter of the Lords of Truth	Daughter of the Flaming Sword, Prophet of the Eternal
XII Hanged Man	Spirit of the Powers of Water, the One Who Hangs Between Heaven and Earth	Spirit of the Mighty Water, Child of the Great Transformers
XIII Death	Lord of the Gate of Death, Child of the Great Transformers	Lord of the Gate of Death, Daughter of the Reconcilers
XIV Temperance	Daughter of Reconciliation, Light of the Door of Life	Bringer-Forth of Life, Lord of the Gates of Matter

FIG. 8. *The magical titles of the Major Arcana*

XV Devil	Lord of the Gates of Matter, Son of the Forces of Time	Child of the Forces of Time
XVI Lightning-Struck Tower	Lord of Proud Armies	Lord of the Hosts of the Mighty, Daughter of the Firmament
XVII Star	Daughter of the Firmament, That Which Lives between the Waters	Dweller Between the Waters, Ruler of Flux and Reflux
XVIII Moon	Master of the Marches; Ebb, the Flood & the Salt Sea	Child of the Sons of the Mighty
XIX Sun	Master of the Fire of the Worlds	Lord of the Fire of the World
XX Judgement	Spirit of Primordial Fire	Spirit of the Primal Fire
XXI Fool	Genius of Transformation	Spirit of Aether
XXII World	Lord of the Night of Time	Great One of the Night of Timt

FIG. 8. *The magical titles of the Major Arcana (cont'd)*

These magical titles give ample opportunity for meditation. In a quiet and undisturbed place, take one card, setting it up before you, familiarize yourself with its image. Address the figure on the card by its title and ask to enter its realm, for example, the Moon: "O Master of the Marches, lead me between the ebb and flow of the salt sea, that I may contemplate your mystery." Enter the card in imagination, be aware of what you are shown. Return and make notes, thanking the figure of the card with "I thank you, O Master of the Marches. May your mystery be revealed within my soul." Return to ordinary consciousness and put the card back in the deck.

THE ROYAL ROAD AND THE SEVEN VEILS OF INITIATION

How is the Tarot "a complete teaching of the Seven Veils of Initiation"? The seven veils that Rolt-Wheeler writes about in his work originate in the Mesopotamian myth of the goddess, the Sumerian Inanna, later worshipped as Ishtar by the Akkadians, Babylonians, and Assyrians. Her myth speaks of her descent into the underworld, which is accomplished by her having to give up one of her attributes at each of its gates. These attributes correspond not only with parts of the body but also with the seven levels of the Tree of Life, which are the "seven veils." We can see how the Assyrian myth and the sephiroth of the Tree correspond to each other, revealing the initiatory way (Lehtu).

In the myth, Ishtar is stripped utterly naked and hung on a hook, like the Hanged Man, undergoing suffering until she is released and able to claim back her attributes one by one. Significantly, Ishtar's symbol is the eight-pointed star, which in many Tarots in depicted upon the Star card, because Ishtar becomes

Ishtar Give Up	From Her Body	The sevenfold Ladder of Initiation
Crown	head	Kether
Earrings	ears	Chokmah & Binah
Necklace	neck	Daath
Brooches	chest	Chesed & Geburah
Belt	waist	Tiphareth
Ankle bracelets	ankles	Netzach and Hod
Her garment	her whole body	Yesod & Malkuth

FIG. 9. *The sevenfold Ladder of Initiation in the Myth of Ishtar*

the mistress of the eighth level after her descent and reascent, which can be seen as a model for initiation. She has risen above the seven veils or levels and, like the Shekinah that followed humanity out of paradise into the world of manifestation, she shines upon the path of all who follow the initiatory way. Anyone stepping upon the initiatory path may presume that this "royal way" of initiation, as Rolt-Wheeler calls it, is going to be a series of wondrous elevations and enlightenments. After a brief attempt, it is clear that there is a lot of material luggage to off-load first, and that initiation requires us to clarify our lives before any elevations come our way. This is not about ritual humiliation but rather about self-knowledge.

The sevenfold ladder of the sephiroth leads us from level to level; as we clarify our daily lives on the material plane, we enter into the royal way that elevates our souls, for we are ascending and descending at the same time in order to mediate heaven to earth and earth to heaven.

> Through Kether, we seek spiritual light that confers the Cosmic Crown of Ever-lasting Life upon us.
>
> Through Chokmah, we dedicate ourselves to the attainment of Wisdom.
>
> Through Binah, we approach the Mysteries with humility in order to receive the revelation Understanding.
>
> Through Chesed, we mediate the Mercy of the Divine to all, caring for our fellow beings with compassion.
>
> Through Geburah, we Discipline ourselves so that we live responsibly and harm none.
>
> Through Tiphareth, we strive to live in Harmony and accord.
>
> Through Netzach, we Persevere with faith and Endure despite all difficulties.

Through Hod, we study the Mysteries with Respect and Reason.

Through Yesod, we practice the principles that are the Foundation of the Mysteries.

Through Malkuth, we keep the laws of the Kingdom of earth that we may enter into its Sovereignty as initiated members of the Mysteries.

These are the true adornments of the initiate: not a collection of ritual equipment or personal emblems, but the inner wisdom that the path teaches us. May the ever-flowing attributes of the Tree enable your Tarot studies, as you set your feet upon the royal road of initiation!

CHAPTER 4

TAROT MÉDIÉVAL IN ACTION

Practical Divination

Throughout his writing, Rolt-Wheeler stresses that the major arcana should not be used for divination except when looking at issues of principles or tendencies: in this warning, he understands the major arcana to have a more elevated quality than the minor arcana. To fully underscore this assertion, the author provides a dominant meaning to each card, but then gives the reader the more usual meanings that would be used in divination, except for the World card, which is exempted. At least Rolt-Wheeler was not reluctant to engage with the cards in a practical divinatory way, like Oswald Wirth who had originally set aside all thoughts of practical divination until after his own Tarot came out, when all his friends clamored for readings! This neglect was something that Wirth remedied when the second edition of his Tarot was published.

Modern readers may find a reluctance to use the major arcana bewildering, but some cartomancers in the past actually resisted using the major arcana in questions of everyday concern, since it meant that cards like the Devil, the Tower, and the Hanged Man might come into the reading, as well as the greater influence of the other trumps, and thus throw a reading "out of scale" with the question's more mundane concerns. This question of "scale" is something that new Tarot readers often encounter when casting a few cards when asking an ordinary question about the week's events, only to be confronted by Death, Justice, and a reversed

Hierophant! The minor arcana do address the ordinary everyday details, and there is nothing wrong in separating them from the major arcana and drawing a few minor cards for the substance of the question, but just one major card for a guidance to determine under which the influence that the question falls.

Although Rolt-Wheeler was himself chiefly interested in the Tarot's initiatory and magical qualities, as we have already seen, in this chapter we will explore the practical divinatory aspects of the whole Tarot Médiéval, as well as considering the art of reading with pip cards.

READING WITH PIP CARDS

Since the minor arcana number cards of Tarot Médiéval have only the number of their emblems on each card, those readers unused to pip cards without any illustration will find it necessary to read in a different style. When the visual clues are not present, the number and suit of the card take on a much greater significance in helping us to interpret. The following method of reading is an older and more cartomantic way, drawing upon understandings of the suit, the number of the card, or its rank. If you would rather follow this method, you will find it serves you well with any Tarot with which you are unfamiliar, especially if it has pip cards rather than illustrated ones.

Because Tarot Médiéval is an esoteric Tarot, we can assign each number and suit to the Tree of Life and reckon things by means of the 10 sephiroth and the 4 worlds. Here are some suggestive keywords that show both the expansive and restrictive sides of each card through the focus of each sephira: we cannot truly speak of the sephiroth in the negative, since they are divine attributes that flow to us, but we can recognize the absence of their influence upon our lives and in our actions, or when we fail to be responsive to their promptings.

By combining the template above with the four suits one below, a more flexible way of reading can be discovered by amalgamating keywords according to the context of the question. For example, 5 Swords upright in a reading about improving health: discipline + energetic = exercise. Five Swords reversed in a reading about political action: forceful + struggle = an uprising. However, in a question about how to deal with an ex-partner's intransigence, 5 Swords might well be read as bringing your innate sense of justice to bear upon the ex's dominating tendencies. By allowing the question to lead the cards, you will read in a much more flexible and dynamic manner.

Again, we need to remember that Rolt-Wheeler has swapped round the suit meanings of Swords to accord with fire, rather than air, and the meaning of Scepters or Wands to accord with air, rather than fire, which may be disconcerting if you are used to the other way round!

NO	SEPHIRA:	TOPICS
Ace	KETHER	Beginnings, way-showing, motivation, leading. Failure to emerge, blocking, beguiling, straggling.
2	CHOKMAH	Wisdom, meeting, dialogue, transaction. Meaninglessness, parting, ignoring, withholding.
3	BINAH	Understanding, growth, emerging, fostering. Incomprehension, barrenness, retiring, carelessness.
4	CHESED	Power, order, conservation, encouragement. Weakness, disarray, neglect, condemn.
5	GEBURAH	Justice, adapting, endeavor, discipline. Judgement, inflexible, struggle, punishment.
6	TIPHARETH	Harmony, love, health, balance. Discordance, neglect, affliction, instablity.
7	NETZACH	Victory, opportunity, endurance, faith. Lost opportunity, lack of perseverance, assumption.
8	HOD	Intelligence, consolidation, reason, reassessment. Disjointedness, restlessness, superstition, dissatisfaction.
9	YESOD	Creative foundation, vision, flow, consolidation. Overambition, Illusion, overspill, disappointment.
10	MALKUTH	Kingdom, manifestation, abundance, completion. Dispossession, failure, dearth, dissolution.

FIG. 10. *Hints for reading the pips from the ten Sephiroth*

When you draw a line or run of cards and find cards of the same suit that diminish or increase in number (e.g., 2 Scepters followed by 8 Scepters), then something is becoming more ambitious or more dominant in your reading: similarly, if you have 9 Shekels followed by 3 Shekels, then there is usually less money or resources available for whatever you planned.

Similarly, drawing two to four cards of the same number in a reading also intensifies what the cards are talking about: so, if you have three cards numbered 4, they will speak about how orderly everything is or, if they are reversed, in what a weak condition things are. If you draw just three sets of the same number, notice which suit is missing—this is often very revealing, as the missing suit is sometimes the factor that is missing from the question too. So, if in a reading about finishing a creative project you drew all the threes except the 3 Swords, you might well lack the energy to complete it.

SUITS	KEYWORDS AND QUALITIES:
SWORDS Fire	Creative, passionate, intuitive outgoing, energetic, sociable, impulsive, dominating, reactive, gregarious, technical, force
SCEPTERS Air	Rational, aggressive, thoughtful, ambitious, analytical, discerning, intellectual, incisive, scientific, cruel
CUPS Water	Devoted, responsive, emotional, romantic, loving, yearning, generous, intimate, artistic, heartless, moody, compassionate
SHEKELS Earth	Physical, material, sensuous, cautious, secure, experience, financial, possessive, pragmatic, mercenary, prudent, moderate

FIG. 11. *Keywords and qualities of the suits*

READING THE COURT CARDS

Court cards are mostly read as people in divination, but they can also show modalities and other qualities. Remember, too, that the courts can describe any human being. Again, you can combine the suit qualities above with the roles of the Court cards if you want to be more flexible.

COURT CARDS	ROLES AND MODALITIES
KING	Authoritative, commanding, experienced, prudent, bringing order, patronage. Unbending, exacting, oppressive, forceful, punitive.
QUEEN	Gracious, encouraging, civilizing, mature, generous, moderating & mediating. Demanding, judgemental, indiscriminate, self-centered, lofty.
KNIGHT	Active, wide-ranging, chivalrous, adventurous, dynamic, progressive, independent. Self-indulgent, immoderate, impatient, careless, endangering.
PAGE	Helping, supporting, learning, connecting, youthful, serviceable. Slothful, disobedient, obsequious, boorish, workaholic.

FIG. 12. *Roles and modalities of the court cards*

By combining the Court card roles and modalities with the keywords of each suit, you can find your own ways of reading the Court Cards: so in a question about the true personality of your upcoming date, an upright Knight of Cups can be read as a chivalrous and devoted person; while in a question about a distant friend's unaccountable silence, a reversed Queen of Shekels might be read as someone who is too immersed in the daily round to respond to you at present.

A Note on Reversals and unfavorable cards

Many people shy away from using card reversals, but when a helpful or positive card appears on a less favorable position, or when it is not showing its full helpfulness, you have the power to consult the unfavorable or reversed meanings. For example, in a question about promoting your work, you find you have laid the Sun upon a position signifying what is detrimental to it. Scrutinize what you are being told: perhaps your promotion will overexpose your business methods, or spotlight your product in a negative light, or that you will not enjoy unalloyed success all the way to the bank. Also, when you have laid a card that you cannot easily interpret in relation to your question, try turning to the reversed meanings to see if they unlock the meaning.

Reading directly and in sequence

In historical Tarot reading before the modern era, all court cards were shown facing in one direction or another, and rarely or never facing forward. Modern Tarots now have many forward-facing cards—something that would have seemed very confrontative to our ancestors. We live in an era when Tarot has become highly psychologized, of course, and reading with cards looking directly at us is not such a problem for us, for we are more easily able to comprehend the cards psychologically as aspects of ourselves or of others. In Tarot Médiéval, a majority of the court cards face to one side or another, meaning that when another card is placed next to them, the figure on the card seems to consider it or turn its back upon it: this kind of sequence-reading enables us to interpret, especially if we choose to read cards in lines, as an unfolding sequence.

The Court cards in *Tarot Médiéval* look like this, directionally speaking.

The Directionality of the Court Cards:

Page of Scepters: walking to left, looking right,
    holding a scroll
Page of Swords: facing behind to left, holding up a torch
Page of Cups: walking to right with veiled chalice Page of
Shekels: seated facing right, shackled in prison

Knight of Scepters, facing right, a flowering branch
Knight of Swords, facing right: a sword with its tip
    downward
Knight of Cups, facing left: a chalice or cup
Knight of Shekels, facing left: a coin with a cross of four
arrows pointing outward

Queen of Scepters: facing forward, holding up her scepter
Queen of Swords: facing to the left, in full armor
Queen of Cups: facing right, holding a veiled chalice
Queen of Shekels: facing forward, holding a large coin

King of Scepters: seated facing left, holding his scepter
King of Swords: seated facing forward, holding his sword
King of Cups: seated facing forward, holding a veiled
    chalice
King of Shekels: standing, facing forward, holding
    a large coin

To see how this works in practice, here is an example where the Page of Scepters is looking at the card on the right, while his feet are walking to the left: we may read that the Page of Scepters brings a gift as a peace offering after being misunderstood, perhaps, as reversed Star behind him shows the misunderstanding, and 4 Shekels is his peace offering. Or it might show that he has been intercepted or diverted from completing an action or receiving a reward because of some lack of faith in him.

FIG. 13. *Example of a directional reading*

In this method of reading, you can also read a court card or major arcana card when it faces you full on and you would like it to tell you more: try placing one card over it and one card under it. In a major arcana card like Justice, the card laid over its head will show how Justice will be served, while the card under its feet will show what needs to be brought into balance. In the case of a court card, the card overhead will reveal what a person is primarily thinking about or intending to do in relation to your question, while the card beneath it reveals what they are not seeing or less inclined to do.

To the left is an example of a question concerning the likelihood of the bank giving you a loan for your house extension. We read that this is unlikely or at least difficult: the forward-facing Queen of Shekels stands for the banker, 2 Swords is about mutual benefit and helping those who are weak, while reversed Judgement is a lost cause,

FIG. 14. *Directional reading with forward-facing cards*

or a situation requiring more scrutiny. The banker might be inclined to help you, but looking at the erratic state of your account, she might require you to prove you can pay back any loan.

SPEAKING THE CARDS

Many taromancers today read each card separately, often in relation to a positional meaning, but the older method is to read the cards in sequence, or as shorter statements, by merging one card with the next. The father of all cartomancy, Etteilla, spoke of a previous card "falling upon" the following card, which in turn "fell upon"—or we would say—"merges with" the next card. We are familiar with this method in its pictorial form from the storyboard of a shooting script, where a film director will work from a cartoon strip of pictures that show the action, sequence, and camera angle, all drawn by an artist, so that the whole crew know how the scene is to be shot.

In Tarot terms, we lay cards in a line and speak the sense of each card, merging it with the following cards to create a statement or sentence. Here is a line of cards where we are asking about a very late payment due on a project for which someone has done a lot of advance work. He asks, "What is causing the unconscionable delay on this payment?"

  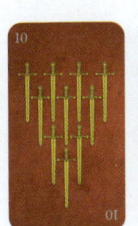  

"The abundance you were expecting (Empress), is delayed—probably due to the loss of a legal case (reversed Chariot), which has caused bankruptcy (10 Swords). Your payment's failure to arrive (reversed 5 Shekels) is resultant from the company's downfall (Tower.)"

This was unfortunately the case: the company paying the man had gone up against a competitor who took them to court, tying up their finances as bankruptcy followed on the firm losing the case. He is still waiting for his money.

This method of reading deepens the practical information that the taromancer is conveying by means of the cards, as a story unfolds from the sequence of the cards. It is this very storytelling that lies at the heart of a good divination.

READING THE STORY

Reading the Story is one of the simplest ways of reading. Compose your question and lay 5 cards—I have shown them here in an arrowhead formation for ease of explanation. Read cards 1–5 as a sequence, as if they were telling you a story. Read 6 as a confirmation of the reading. There are no individual position meanings because the cards are like pages in a book. If you want to search more deeply, you can read the mirrored pairs to help reveal the dynamic of the story, by pairing card 1 with 5, and card 2 with 4. Reading cards 3 with 6 together will give you the last word.

In figure 16, we have an example where Strength, Hanged Man, 2 Cups, 6 Swords, and Queen of Swords are drawn sequentially, with Empress as the confirmation card.

FIG. 15. *Reading the story*

We notice also the directionality of the cards—with Strength and Queen Swords looking to the left and Hanged Man and Empress facing forward.

FIG. 16. *Example of reading the story*

The question is, "How will the launch of the new project play out?" The sequence reads: "You need the courage and dedication to bring together the plan and the customers. The way forward is through personal effort and oversight." The confirmation card tells us, "The project will be manifested." To find the internal dynamic, we read the cards together as pairs: "A strong woman does the project alone" (cards 1 + 5); "It will take a dedicated approach in which there may be delays" (cards 2 + 4); "The power to harmonize the project and its potential users is clearly present."

THE JUDGEMENT OR FRENCH CROSS SPREAD

This spread was first printed in Oswald Wirth's 1927 book *Le Tarot des Imagiers du Moyen Age* (Tarot of the Medieval Crafts-People), and is usually known as "the French Cross" today. It is in traditional Tarot repertoire today, but this spread is not quite one hundred years old, so speedily do we assimilate divinatory influences! The cards are spread as if they were in a courtroom, with advocates who are for and against the consultant's question, with an impartial judge, and a decision at the end of it. The fifth card represents a synthesis of all the other cards linked together.

METHOD:

1. The consultant asks a question, ensuring that it is not one that would result in a yes/no answer. The vaguer the question, the vaguer will be the answer; the more exact the question, the more exact the answer will be, so it is worth composing your question carefully.
2. The original version of this spread uses just the major cards, but I have suggested variants below. Wirth also had the consultant giving the reader a number between 1-22 to select the cards, but that was in an era when people didn't know Tarot well, so today, you can select your 22 major arcana by shuffling and drawing them.

FIG. 17. *The Judgement or French Cross spread*

3. Select unseen 4 major arcana cards and lay them upon the following positions:

   Position 1 represents the favorable and positive aspects of the question: what it would be wise to do, pointing to helpful people or elements that would support it.

   Position 2 represents what is unfavorable, revealing the negative aspects of the question: the dangers, enemies, the faults in the plan, the tendencies that are bearing it off course.

   Position 3 is the impartiality of discussion or debate: how to decide or resolve the question, what interventions it requires.

   Position 4 is the sentence pronounced upon the question:
   what results from the discussion. This is the final result.

4. Finally, add up the numerical values of the cards drawn, reducing them to give you a number between 1 and 23. For example, Temperance, Emperor, Star, Judgement have values of 14 + 4 + 17 + 20 = 55. Adding the total values together (if they are not already below 23), we have 5 + 5 = 10 of Wheel of Fortune. Note: this method of "Theosophical

addition" or "Quintessence" can result in one of the cards already used coming out again as the total.
5. Position 5 gives us the synthesis that links all the cards together: it may contain more information or elucidation, but position 4 remains the result.

Alternative Methods: You can also use the full set of cards for this cross, using the instruction as above: in which case, you will be adding the face value of each card on positions 1–4, with Page as 11, Knight as 12, Queen as 13, and King as 14. Alternatively, you can lay an additional line of three extra cards that are read as your passport to the next step.

FIG. 18. *An example of Judgement spread*

Here, Jerry considers his retirement from teaching: he really wants to ask, "Is this the right time to retire?" but realizes this is a yes/no question, so he modifies it to, "Show me how to judge when is best to retire."

1. For him is the V Pope: The Pope is the card of instruction and teaching, and shows Jerry doing what he loves best, as he is a teacher.
2. Against him is III Empress: the constant struggle to manifest new ideas and fresh teaching models is becoming onerous to him.
3. The question's Judge is XVII Star, which speaks of the good work and service Jerry has given, as well as of his growing pessimism with it.
4. The solution is reversed XX Judgement: while Jerry could return to the workplace, he is more than ready to retire now.
5. The synthesis is arrived at by adding the numbers of each card drawn together: 5 +3 + 17 + 20 = 45. The total of 4 + 5 is added together = 9 or Hermit: Jerry's solution is underscored, confirming his time of retreat is already nigh.

WEFT OF THE MYSTERIES SPREAD

Rolt-Wheeler speaks warmly of the geometric shape of the lozenge as a symbol of the involutionary and evolutionary powers, so here is a spread in his honor, respecting his understanding of the Tarot as a tool of the mysteries, enabling you to seek guidance and insight. You can consult the method from steps 1–4 as a basic process. If you want more insight, continue with steps 5–10.

POSITION MEANINGS:

1. The Wise Guide: shows an approach you may not be considering.
2. The Companion: shows the power or virtue that will be of help for you to deploy.

3. The Opener of the Way: shows an opening or opportunity that is near.
4. The Keeper of the Secret: shows where you need to be reserved or cautious.
5. What is inherited: the history or context of the issue, factors/people who may still be resonating or influencing.
6. What is new-born: the yet unsaid or unthought truth of the issue, factors/people who can cast light on it.
7. What is required: an essential skill to use, or factors/people who are part of the issue.
8. What is to be left: the inessential aspects to leave behind, factors/people who muddle the issue.
9. The gift at the point of departure: powers/factors/people—see step 3 in the method below.

FIG. 19. *Weft of the Mysteries spread*

WEFT OF THE MYSTERIES METHOD:

Consider your issue and make a statement of it:

1. Separate your major arcana cards from the minors. Shuffle them together while posing the question, "What advice is given to guide me through this issue?" Lay one major arcana each, unseen, upon positions 1, 2, 3, and 4.
2. Shuffle the minor arcana with the court cards, asking, "What factors or people will I meet as deal with this issue?" Lay one minor arcana or court card upon positions 5, 6, 7, and 8. Cards 1-10 show actions/events. Courts show people/qualities.
3. Combine your unused cards into one pack and shuffle it. Draw one unseen card to lay upon position 9. A major arcana card will speak the wisdom you need to hear. A minor arcana card will indicate the next step. A court card will direct you to the elemental power or person that you require in resolving or accomplishing your issue.
4. Read your cards, consider your advice, and the factors or people that are in the mix with your issue. Read position 9 as the next step or the question to ponder.
5. If you would like to take the reading further, you can also read the cards at another level, examining the four crosses formed by the cards: you are going to be reading each cross as a story or mystery of its own. Be aware that a card that you have read in one cross will appear in one or more of the other four crosses, but try and make the story from each of the four cards, ignoring all the positional meanings.
6. Northern Cross: made up of cards 1, 5, 6, 9. What started this story?
7. Eastern Cross: made up of cards 6, 9, 3, 7. What factors wove it together?
8. Southern Cross: made up of cards 9, 8, 7, 2. What is still playing out?
9. Western Cross: made up of cards 5, 4, 9, 8. What is still to be accomplished?
10. From the stories you have told, what do you now know about the issue? What steps do you take? What movements/ changes feel possible?

Here, Chloe is embroiled in a collaborative project. When she started it, its prospects looked wonderful, but now things feel muddled and conflicted. Her question is, "Please reveal the project in its true light, so I can make good choices about it."

FIG. 20. *Example of the Weft of the Mysteries*

1. XIX The Sun is her Wise Guide, which is speaking about the lessening of energy in the whole project.
2. Reversed XX Judgement is her Companion, suggests that the project is a lost cause, and that Chloe needs liberation from it, as it is like a stone around her neck: there is no resuscitation possible.
3. Her Opener of the Ways is IX the Hermit, suggesting that she take the opportunity to withdraw.
4. XI Strength is her Keeper of the Secret and cautions her against a possible abuse of power. It is time to conserve her powers.
5. Ten Cups shows what this project has inherited: a scrambling after the top award is driving it, but it feels to Chloe that this has been wiping out all other considerations
6. Page of Shekels reveals the unspoken factor: the naked pursuit of profit.
7. Ace of Swords shows what this project requires: a ruthlessness of mind that Chloe does not possess or want to emulate.
8. Two of Scepters reveals that these burdensome responsibilities need to be left behind.
9. Knight of Scepters underscores the truth that this project has a wild trajectory that will most likely pull Chloe under its chariot wheels. Scepters represent the element of air: it is necessary for her to hold her integrity closely to her so that she is not tainted by the way this project is working out.

Chloe gets the message clearly, but she makes an attempt to read each cross as a story, as she feels a growing reluctance to give up her part of the collaboration. She writes down her own findings:

Northern Cross: Sun, 10 Cups, Page Shekels, Knight of Scepters: "It all started out with the best of intentions, but now profit and gain are making the project unpredictable." Southern Cross: Knight Scepters, 2 Scepters, Ace Swords, and reversed Judgement: "The project careers on in an unbalanced way, and everyone is trying to grab control, but I want to withdraw before

I become one of the living dead."

Eastern Cross: Page Shekels, Knight of Scepters, Hermit, Ace of Swords: "Money is the driving consideration here, and it is brutalizing my attempt to develop any ideas quietly and with integrity."

Western Cross: 10 Cups, Strength, Knight of Scepters, 2 Scepters: "My collaborators have the big prizes in their sights, and the best I can do is to look after myself or be pulled into their aggressive game, where I will be tempted to overlook the real value of the idea."

Outcome: Chloe took the opportunity of a long public holiday to withdraw from the project, which had begun to get out of hand. She rightly feared the anger of her collaborators, but her relief on laying the whole thing down was so considerable, she knew she had made the right decision. You can see here how many of the upright cards are behaving in what Rolt-Wheeler calls "an unfavorable way," which is why Chloe read them as if they had been reversed.

QUESTIONS OF TIMING

Timing questions are the most difficult to answer, but you can use the court cards to reveal a rough timing of an event. Decide which kind of spread or reading is suitable for your question, read on the issue, and then shuffle all the cards from your spread together. Cut the deck into two piles. Turn over the cards from the pack one, one at a time—the first Page you turn over will reveal the season. Then turn over the cards one at a time from pack two, the first Knight, Queen, or King will reveal the date. If you've had no court cards whatever in your reading, use the full deck to do this. Be aware that timing questions rarely give more than 64 percent accuracy to any question, in my experience, although the date given may reveal a significant development concerning your question. Here are the correspondences of the Pages to the Seasons:

PAGE: SEASON:

Page of Shekels	Spring—from March to May
Page of Wands	Summer—from June to August
Page of Cups	Autumn—from September to November
Page of Scepters	Winter—from December to February

TIME OF THE YEAR	COURT CARDS
March 11–April 9	Queen of Wands
April 10–May 10	King of Shekels
May 11–June 10	Knight of Swords
June 11–July 12	Queen of Cups
July 13–August 12	King of Wands
August 13–September 12	Knight of Shekels
September 13–October 13	Queen of Swords
October 14–November 12	King of Cups
November 13–December 11	Knight of Wands
December 12–January 10	Queen of Shekels
January 11–February 8	King of Swords
February 9–March 10	Knight of Cups

FIG. 21 *The Knights, Queens, and Kings reveal the date*

BEING LED BY THE CARDS, THROUGH THE LIGHT OF THE MYSTERIES

Every Tarot comes with its own aesthetic and concepts, but its cards truly only come alive when the reader plays with them daily, finding just how they interrelate with each other, and how certain cards and their combinations reveal meaning. Becoming familiar with your cards starts with drawing a handful every day and making a note of what you feel they are showing you. Look at them later, at the end of the day, considering how that day played out in reality; note which cards and combinations of cards revealed particular insights.

The images upon the cards are like stepping stones leading to the concepts behind them, so that our growing understanding may begin to use them as guides to our daily and spiritual lives also. They will take you into your personal style of reading, one that also serves your own spiritual life, which is how we are led to the mysteries of the initiate's path.

Tarot Médiéval is a Tarot conceived in another era, but it can still show us its mysteries for our own times. As Rolt-Wheeler wrote in his 1935 article on "The Recurrence of the Ancient Rites": "every age is inspired by its religion, each era is inspired by its mysteries, and progress never stops. . . . Those who wish to establish an esoteric renaissance upon an ancient foundation try valiantly to bring back old-fashioned rituals by means of modern interpretations that ill-accord with the original ancient rites." To progress, the mysteries "have no need of theatricals, nor any creased hierophantic garb . . . nor would we want to resuscitate bloody sacrifices, nor the dances of masked gods, which are in the past."[24]

He speaks too of the many organizations that were trying to restore the Mysteries on modern lines in the 1930s—the era of Dion Fortune and other eminent magicians and thinkers who shaped the magical development of our time—and he asks, "Is it truly possible to reestablish esoteric rites in our own day? . . . The true esoteric mysteries of the future will follow the development of the mind which is the characteristic of our age, whereby they will pass from the concrete into the abstract. . . . The sign of a true mystery tradition is discerned by whatever enables our individualization, by whatever inspired rituals are worthy of our era and our progress. . . . The Mysteries of our ages lie before us, not behind us."[25]

Writing nearly ninety years and four generations after Rolt-Wheeler wrote these words before World War II, I invite you to consider the mysteries by which you lead your own life: the great myths and stories, the uplifting themes and movements that have shaped your own development, and to consider the unknown path that stretches still ahead of you. What legacy will you leave for future generations, what from your studies and meditations will inspire them and reveal unfolding mysteries for ages to come?

May the light of the unfolding mysteries shine ever upon your path!

GLOSSARY

I have glossed esoteric, mythic, and other specialist terms used by Rolt-Wheeler in Tarot Médiéval for ease of understanding. Terms that cross-refer are in italic.

ABSOLUTE: The absolute is the fullest understanding of the whole of a principle, indicating the unknowable divine, in this book.

ADAM KADMON: The Cosmic Man of the *Tree of Life*: the combined *sephiroth* together make up the spiritual body of Adam Kadmon.

AIN, AIN SOPH, and AIN SOPH AUR: Kabbalistic terms for, respectively, "nothing," "limitlessness," and "the unending light." These three preexistent essences are the source from which all ten *sephiroth* emanate.

ALCHEMY: The process by which seekers come to harmonize their essential nature. It also applies to the chemical processes of purification and essentialization of raw materials, metals, and substances, and their transmutation into gold.

APOLLONIUS OF TYANA: A first-century BCE Neo-Pythagorean philosopher and wonderworker whose wisdom was influential both in Classical times and in Hermetic magic. He traveled widely in the East with his companion, Damis; both were recognized in Sanskrit sources as Western yogic practitioners.

ARCANA: The secrets or mysteries. Rolt-Wheeler often refers to individual cards as "this arcana."

ASSIAH: The fourth of the kabbalistic worlds concerned with the principle of manifestation; the manifestation of creation in physical form.

ASTROLOGY, ESOTERIC, and EXOTERIC: Two different methods of astrology coexist: "esoteric astrology" refers to the progress of the soul and to spiritual evolution, wherein the author connects each card and the mysteries implicit within it; he uses "exoteric astrology" to refer to the planetary relationships of the card as they apply to classical astrological computation of personality and identity.

ATZILUTH: The first of the kabbalistic worlds concerned with the principle of emanation, the intention behind all creation.

BAPHOMET: The being that the Knight's Templars were accused of worshipping in 1307. It was further popularized by Éliphas Lévi in his nineteenth-century books of magic, where he suggested it had been the being worshipped at the witches' sabbat.

BINAH: Understanding is the third sephira on the *Tree of Life*.

BLAZON: The heraldic emblem or symbol upon a knight's shield.

BOAZ and JACHIN: The two pillars of the Solomonic Temple; they are also seen on the Priestess card. The left-hand pillar from Binah to Hod is seen as the Pillar of Severity or contraction, while the right-hand pillar from Chokmah to Netzach is seen as the Pillar of Mercy or expansion.

BRIAH: The second of the kabbalistic worlds concerned with the principle of creation—providing the primal impulse for creation.

CHESED: Loving-kindness is the fourth sephira on the *Tree of Life*.

CHOKMAH: Wisdom is the second sephira on the *Tree of Life*.

CUBIC STONE: A metaphor of the perfected initiate. In Revelation 21, the new Jerusalem is described as a perfect cube, as is the Holy of Holies in the Temple of Jerusalem.

DECANS: These are the ten-degree arcs of the ecliptic, or the path of the earth's orbit about the sun: in effect, the decans divide each sign of the zodiac into three parts, making 36 decans in all. The Golden Dawn system allots one decan each to the minor arcana cards numbered 2–10. The decans derive from Egyptian and Arabic sources: each decan was accorded a spirit in this system, propitious for undertaking *talismanic magic*.

DEMIURGE: The one who fashions the universe in Platonic and Gnostic philosophy: not the same as the monotheist creator.

ELEMENTS: The Classical elements of air, fire, water, and earth as applied to the four suits of the Tarot.

ESOTERIC: The hidden mysteries of a magical principle that become known to an initiate.

EVOLUTION: The flow of life back to its divine source from earth.

EXOTERIC: The open or received understanding of a magical principle.

FOUR WORLDS: The four worlds of Atziluth, Briah, Yetzirah, and Assiah are the four principles of creation from intention, primal impulse, formation, and manifestation upon the *Tree of Life*.

FREEMASONRY: Having its basis in the confraternal rituals of medieval stone masons, it is the practice of fraternal associates who meet together to inculcate mutual tolerance, charitable works, and the reformation of the character by the practice of truth, virtue, and moral restraint.

GEBURAH: Strength is the fifth sephira on the *Tree of Life*.

GEMATRIA: The Kabbalistic process of assessing the numerical value of words from their individual Hebrew letters and associating them with words of a similar value. For example, Genesis 28:12 speaks of Jacob's dream of a ladder (*sullam*) stretching from earth to heaven: the letters in *sullam* = 130 or 60 + 30 + 40; because Sinai, the mountain where Moses received the tablets of the law, has the same numerical value (Sinai = 130 or 60 + 10 + 50 + 10), 130 is deemed to convey the meaning of "reaching heaven."

GNOSTICS: Literally "knowers." Gnostics were made up of a variety of sects in the early centuries of Christianity, which included proto-Christian, Jewish, Hellenistic Egyptians, and other post-Classical people of spirit, who believed in the multiple spiritual emanations of the divine.

GREAT ARCHITECT OF THE UNIVERSE: A Freemasonic metaphor for the Creator or Divine Being.

GREAT WORK: The summit of the work of Hermetic magic, whereby heaven and earth are brought together in the person of the initiate in such a way that he or she is utterly changed. It is the Western equivalent to the Eastern understanding of "enlightenment," similar to "the making of the soul" within Christian mysticism.

GREATER MYSTERIES: In initiatory parlance, initiation into the Greater Mysteries of a lodge or mystery school enables the initiate to be reformulated by the myth or core belief that sustains the lodge, whereby s/he is able to mediate the principles of its guiding spirit through life. The principle of bringing together and harmonizing heaven with earth, spirit and matter lies at its heart. Arcana 10–19 represent the Greater Mysteries in this Tarot.

HAYYOTH HA KADOSH: The Four Holy Living Creatures who are first seen in the book of Ezekiel 1:5 are described as the supporters of God's throne, each having four faces and four wings: of a man, a lion, an ox, and an eagle. In the book of Revelation 4:6–8, they reappear but now with six wings. In Christian iconography, they have been associated with the Four Evangelists: the man of Matthew, the lion of Mark, the ox of Luke, and the eagle of John, appearing in the same order as on the card of the XXII The World, but with the risen Christ in the center.

HEBREW LETTERS: The letters of the Hebrew alphabet were first associated with the Tarot in the eighteenth century. In Judaism, each letter is understood as a creative sound in its own right, the means by which creation came into being.

HERMANUBIS: A fusion of the Greek god Hermes with the Egyptian god

Anubis that came about in the Hellenic period of Egyptian history; he acts as the guide to the soul.

HERMETIC MAGIC: The study of the universal concepts of magic by which matter and spirit are brought together and harmonized. Hermes/Mercury was seen as the mentor and guardian of these mysteries.

HOD: Glory is the eighth sephira on the *Tree of Life*.

HOLY GRAIL: The Holy Grail is the cup by which peace, healing, and harmony are brought to the earth within mystical Christian myth.

HOUSES: In the meanings of most of the minor arcana cards, the author gives the zodiacal house with which each card is associated.

INITIATION: The process of stepping upon the magical path and entering into its practices. An initiate is someone who has literally "entered within" a spiritual path.

INVISIBLE FRATERNITY: A term that includes the initiates of all forms of initiatory and magical lodges, from all times and ages, including the present and future, which makes a golden chain of connection and responsibility to the principles of the mysteries.

INVOLUTION: The downward flow of life from its heavenly source to earth.

ISIS-URANIA: A fusion of the Egyptian Goddess, Isis, and the Greek Ourania, muse of astronomy, in her aspect of universal teacher.

KABBALISM: The Jewish study of creation, its spiritual understanding and application to daily life.

KETHER: The Crown is the first sephira on the *Tree of Life*.

KLIMAX HEPTAULOS: The sevenfold ladder upon which many magical and mystery schools base their initiatory grades is found in the ancient world, especially in Zoroastrian, Gnostic, and Mithraic traditions. This symbol came into the world via astrology whose study had its roots in Mesopotamia; by overcoming the vices of the seven classical planets of Moon, Mercury, Venus, Sun, Mars, Jupiter, and Saturn, the initiate would progress in the mysteries.

LEMNISCATE: The emblem of power and eternity, shown as a horizonal figure of eight.

LESSER MYSTERIES: In initiatory parlance, initiation into the Lesser Mysteries of a lodge or mystery school enables the initiate to be inculcated into the myth or core belief that sustains the lodge, whereby s/he attunes to its guiding principles and becomes a servant of its guiding gods and archetypes. Arcana 1–9 represent the Lesser Mysteries in this Tarot.

LETHE: The river of forgetfulness in the Greek afterlife.

LOZENGE: A symbol of the *involutionary* and *evolutionary* powers.

MACROCOSM: The greater world of the universe, including all that is unseen.

MAJOR ARCANA: An esoteric way of speaking about the *Trumps* number I–XXII: "major arcana" was a term invented by Paul Christian in the nineteenth century.

MALKUTH: The Kingdom of Sovereignty is the tenth sephira on the *Tree of Life*.

MANDORLA: An almond or oval shape, appearing on the World card.

MICROCOSM: The lesser world of the sublunary sphere, including earth and the moon.

MINOR ARCANA: an esoteric way of speaking about the four suits numbered Ace–10 : a term invented by Paul Christian in the nineteenth century.

NETZACH: Victory is the seventh sephira on the *Tree of Life*.

OCEAN OF CHAOS: The primordial waters from which creation emerged in many mythologies, including that of Greece, and the Middle Eastern mythologies.

PATHS: The thirty-two paths upon the *Tree of Life* connect the ten *sephiroth*, enabling kabbalists to meditate and move in spirit along with them. To each path is assigned a Hebrew letter, though these are not consistent between kabbalists, Qabalists, or different schools of Tarot.

PERENNIAL PHILOSOPHY: The sense that all spiritual traditions point to the same truth.

PETER'S PENCE: Originally an offering begun by King Alfred the Great, who collected money from landowners to support the pope. It is still donated by faithful Catholics for that purpose.

PHILOSOPHER'S STONE: The summit of the work of *alchemy*.

PILLARS—*see Boaz and Jachin.*

PIPS: The numbers cards 1–10 of each Tarot suit: these appear with just the emblems of their suit and without illustrations.

POLARITY: Rolt-Wheeler uses this term to indicate the maleness and femaleness of all things. Also, as the magical principle of giving and receiving, or reciprocation, necessary to transmit life in humans, to convey concepts between pupil and teacher, or to transmit power in a ritual.

QABALA: The magical study of kabbalism by gentiles, whose esoteric tenets are now commonly applied to Tarot cards.

QLIPPOTH: Literally "husk," the evil influences that seek to arrest the soul's journey; the inverse of the holy *sephiroth*, where the husks inhabit a reversed Tree.

QUARTERNITY: A fourfold collective, usually applied to the four elements.

QUINTERNARY/QUINTESSENCE: A fivefold collective, usually applied to the four elements plus spirit.

RELATIVE: The relative is the personal and human understanding of a principle.

RISHIS: The Seven Sages of Hindu belief who are represented by the seven stars of the Plough or Ursa Major.

ROSA MYSTICA: One of the titles of the Blessed Virgin Mary, from the Litany of Loretto.

ROSE CROSS: The rose upon the cross was the emblem of Rosicrucians, an esoteric fellowship founded in seventeenth-century Germany to follow the esoteric Christian mysteries.

SEPHIRAH/SEPHIROTH (singular and plural): A sephirah is one of the vessels of the *Tree of Life*, on which there are ten sephiroth.

SEPHIROTH OF FORMATION: Refers to the seven lower vessels on the Tree of Life: Chesed, Geburah, Tiphareth, Netzach, Hod, Yesod, and Malkuth.

SET/SETH: Originally an Egyptian god of desert storms, Set was the brother of Osiris and Isis, who opposed Osiris, killed and mutilated him. He was also associated with Typhon and polarized as a god of chaos.

SHADDAI: El Shaddai is one of the names of God in Jewish tradition. Although it is often translated as "the Almighty," it is nearer in meaning to "the Wilderness" or "the Mountains." The name is associated with the Hebrew letter "shin," and Shaddai is written on the back of the mezuzah (the door scroll) of Jewish houses, as well as upon the back of all tephillin, the leather boxes strapped to the arms and head of Jews at prayer.

SHEKINAH: The presence of God that accompanied the Israelites as a pillar of fire by night and a pillar of cloud by day; symbolized as a dynamic feminine presence.

SPHINX: Five symbolic elements in the Sphinx: (1) The wings of the eagle: and the learning about spiritual things. (2) The flanks of the bull: and the power to act. (3) The human head: knowing, and the high spheres. (4) The paws of the lion: the ability to seize opportunities for spiritual elevation, but this, we can see, does not rest on a personal basis. (5) The breasts of a young woman: service, and the helping of others along two feminine ways, both vestal and material, so that one can be an agent for the divine will and become attuned to that will.

SUPERNAL SEPHIROTH: The three highest sephiroth: Kether, Chokmah, and Binah

TALISMANIC MAGIC: The art of creating talismans during the appropriate planetary degree for wealth, beauty, good fortune, etc. This kind of magic is found in the highly influential eleventh-century Arabic book, *Picatrix*, and *De Imaginibus* of Thabit Ibn Qurra.

TETRAGRAMMATON: The great sacred name of the Creator in Kabbalah, made up of the Hebrew letters: Yod, Heh, Vau, Heh. Each of these life-giving letters is associated with the *Four Worlds*.

TIPHARETH: Beauty is the sixth sephira on the *Tree of Life*.

TREE OF LIFE: A conceptual representation of the created universe in all its aspects, which is used as a roadmap or "a ladder of lights" for kabbalists to meditate and travel in spirit upon. Upon the Tree hang the ten *sephiroth* and the thirty-two connective paths between them.

TRINITY: The author uses this term for two different things: to indicate the trinity of the *supernal sephiroth*, and also the Holy Trinity of Father, Son, and Holy Spirit, in discussing mystical Christianity.

TRIPLICITIES: The author uses this term to indicate the fourfold divisions of the zodiacal signs into their elemental groupings of Aries, Leo, and Sagittarius for fire; Taurus, Virgo, and Capricorn for earth; Gemini, Libra, and Aquarius for air; and Cancer, Scorpio, and Pisces for water.

TRUMPS: The major arcana of the Tarot numbered from I–XXII. The name "trump" derives from "triumph," which is how each card was seen, as well as from the trumping or taking of tricks in the many games of Tarot within Europe.

TYPHON: Originally, the monstrous opponent of Zeus in Greek myth, Typhon became associated with *Set* in the Hellenic period of Egyptian history.

YESOD: Foundation is the nineth sephira on the *Tree of Life*.

YETZIRAH: The third of the kabbalistic worlds concerned with the principle of formation and the activation of creation.

NOTES

Throughout the notes,
RW = Rolt-Wheeler and CM = Caitlín Matthews

1. The author refers to the book by Falconnier, illustrated by W. O. Wegener, *Les XXII lames hermètiques du tarot divinatoire*, 1896: these illustrations were reused many times, notably in *The Sacred Tarot* by C. E. Zain, made for the Brotherhood of Light in 1936.

2. Enel was the pseudonym of the Egyptologist and polyglot Michel Vladimirovich Skariatine (1883–1963).

3. Dion Fortune's forthcoming book was actually titled, *The Mystical Qabala*, 1935.

4. Book of Daniel, chapter 5.

5. Rolt-Wheeler firmly says, "The World is not used in divination, but the true meaning is the end—not the desired end, but the end which has to come." However, I have supplied meanings here.

6. Ronald Decker, Theirry Depaulis, and Michael Dummett, *A Wicked Pack of Cards* (London: Duckworth, 1996), 199.

7. Translated by CM.

8. Extracted from RW's entry to Page of Shekels.

9. Extracted from RW's entry to Knight of Shekels.

10. Extracted from RW's entry to Queen of Shekels.

11. Extracted from RW's entry to King of Shekels.

12. Translated by CM.

13. According to *the Dream of Scipio* by Macrobius.

14. Thomas Taylor, quoted in Manley P. Hall's *Secret Teaching of All the Ages* (New York: Jeremy P. Tarcher, 2004).

15. Caitlín Matthews, *Untold Tarot: The Lost Art of Reading Ancient Tarots* (Atglen, PA: Schiffer).

16. Oswald Wirth, *Tarot of the Magicians* (San Francisco: Weiser Books, 2012), 5.

17. Decker et al., *Wicked Pack of Cards*, 24.

18. Baba Studio, "Pierre de Lasenic: A Modern Esoteric Soul," Bohemian Magic, accessed March 20, 2021, http://magicbohemia.magic-realist.com/2017/10/23/pierre-de-lasenic-a-modern-esoteric-soul/, quoted with permission.

19. See Caitlín and John Matthews, *Walkers Between the Worlds* (Rochester, NY: Inner Traditions, 2003).

20. Decker et al., *Wicked Pack of Cards*, 58.

21. Ronald Decker, *Esoteric Tarot: Ancient Sources Rediscovered in Hermeticism and Cabalah* (Wheaton, IL: Quest Books, 2013), 270–74; and Joseph Gikatilla, *Gates of Light (Sha'are Orah)*, trans. Avi Weinstein (London: Harper Collins, 1994).

22. Francis Rolt-Wheeler, *Astrosophie* 8, no 1 (July 1935).

23. See Caitlín Matthews, *Untold Tarot*.

24. Francis Rolt-Wheeler, "La Réchute vers let Rites Anciens," *L'Astrosophie* 12, no. 3 (March 1935): 105–10.

25. Ibid.

BIBLIOGRAPHY

Baba Studio. "Pierre de Lasenic: A Modern Esoteric Soul." Bohemian Magic. Accessed March 20, 2021. Pierre de Lasenic. http://magicbohemia.magic-realist.com/2017/10/23/pierre-de-lasenic-a-modern-esoteric-soul/

Christian, Paul. *The History and Practice of Magic* (*Histoire de la Magie*). Translated by James Kirkup and Julian Shaw. London: Forge, 1952.

Curtess, F. Homer, et al. *A Collection of Secret Wisdom from Tarot's Mystical Origins*. New York: St. Martins, 2021.

Decker, Ronald. *The Esoteric Tarot: Ancient Sources Rediscovered in Hermeticism and Cabalah*. Wheaton, IL: Quest Books, 2013.

Decker, Ronald, Thierry Depaulis, and Michael Dummett. *A Wicked Pack of Cards*. London: Duckworth, 1996.

Decker, Ronald, and Michael Dummett. *A History of the Occult Tarot 1870–1970*. London: Duckworth, 2002.

Etteilla. *Jeu de Grand Etteilla*. Paris: Editions Dusserre, 2015.

———. *Manière de se récréer avec le jeu du cartes nommées tarots*. Amsterdam and Paris, 1785.

Fortune, Dion. *The Mystical Qabala*. Newburyport, MA: Weiser, 2022.

Gikatilla, Joseph. *Gates of Light (Sha'are Orah)*. Translated by trans. Avi Weinstein. London: Harper Collins, 1994.

Hall, Manley P. *The Secret Teaching of All the Ages*. New York: Jeremy P. Tarcher, 2004.

Knight, Gareth. *Magical World of the Tarot*. Newburyport, MA: Red Wheel/Weiser, 1996.

Lehto, Otto. "The Seven Veils of Ishtar and the Ten Sefirot of Israel." University of Helsinki. 2009. Accessed April 21, 2021, http://www.ottolehto.com/wp-content/uploads/2014/01/Otto-Lehto-The-Seven-Veils-of-Ishtar-and-the-Ten-Sefirot-of-Israel-1.0.pdf.

Lévi, Éliphas. *The Clavicule of Solomon*. Accessed March 20, 2021. http://misraim3.free.fr/eliphas_levy/clavicules_de_salomon.pdf.

———. *Le Clef des Grands Mystères*. Accessed March 20, 2021, https://archive.org/details/leclefdesgrandsm00lvil

Macrobius. *Commentary on the Dream of Scipio*. New York and London: Columbia University Press, 1952.

Mathers, S. McGregor. *The Book T*. Accessed April 17, 2021. https://www.tarot.org.il/Library/Mathers/Book-T.

Matthews, Caitlín. *Untold Tarot: The Lost Art of Reading Ancient Tarots*. Atglen, PA: Schiffer, 2018.

Matthews, Caitlín and John. *Walkers between Worlds*. Rochester, NY: Inner Traditions, 2003.

Robinson, Yolanda M. *The Revised New Art-Tarot: Mysticism and Qabalah in the Knapp Hall Tarot*. (no place) CreateSpace, 2015.

Rolt-Wheeler, Francis. *Le Cabbalisme Initiatique* 3 vols. Nice, France: L'Editions Astrosophie, 1936–40.

Rolt-Wheeler, Francis. "L'Extase et la Sagesse." *L'Astrosophie* 8, no. 1 (July 1935): 11–15.

———. "La Réchute vers les Rites Anciens," *L'Astrosophie* 12, no. 3 (March 1935): 105–10.

———. *Mystic Gleams from the Holy Grail*. London: Rider, 1948.

———. *Tarot Médiéval*. Nice, France: Editions Astrosophie 1939.

Williams, Charles. *The Greater Trumps*. London: Faber & Faber, 1932.

Wirth, Oswald. *Tarot of the Magicians*. San Francisco: Weiser Books, 2012.

SOME OSWALD WIRTH–STYLE TAROTS

Kazanlar, Emil. *The Kazanlar Tarot*. Neuhausen, Switzerland: AGM Agmüller, 1996.

Knapp, J. A., and Manley P. Hall. *The Revised New Art Cards*. Los Angeles: Philosophical Research Society, 2013.

Lasenic, Pierre de (Petr Kohout z Lasenice). *Tarot, klic k iniciaci* (*Tarot: Keys of Initiation*). Prague: 1938.

Wirth, Oswald. *Le Tarot des Imagiers du Moyen Age*. Paris: Tchou, 1984.

ABOUT THE AUTHOR AND ILLUSTRATOR

CAITLÍN MATTHEWS is the author of many books on the art of divination, including *Untold Tarot: The Lost Art of Reading Ancient Tarots*, the *Da Vinci Enigma Tarot*, *The Art of Celtic Seership*, and *The Complete Lenormand Oracle Handbook*. She teaches internationally, appearing regularly at Tarot conferences worldwide. Caitlín has spent a lifetime working within the native and hermetic mysteries of the Western esoteric tradition. She is the director of studies for the Foundation for Inspirational and Oracular Studies, which is dedicated to the sacred arts, the oral and mythic traditions, and to ancient sources of inspiration. She has a shamanic practice in Oxford. www.hallowquest.org.uk.

WIL KINGHAN is an artist and writer living in Oxford, UK. He has been many things in his life, from a barman and postie, to a futurist and shamanic practitioner. Growing up in the Ireland of the troubles, his work often explores the borderland between worlds and the dark and light sides of life. Wil has worked on a number of Tarot projects with friends and collaborators John and Caitlín Matthews, including *The Shaman's Oracle*, *The Steampunk Tarot* and, most recently, *The Circle of the Sidhe*.